From Sanctuary to Boardroom

From Sanctuary to Boardroom

A Jewish Approach to Leadership

Hal M. Lewis

ROWMAN & LITTLEFIELD PUBLISHERS, INC.
Lanham • Boulder • New York • Toronto • Oxford

ROWMAN & LITTLEFIELD PUBLISHERS, INC.

Published in the United States of America
by Rowman & Littlefield Publishers, Inc.
A wholly owned subsidary of The Rowman & Littlefield Publishing Group, Inc.
4501 Forbes Boulevard, Suite 200, Lanham, Maryland 20706
www.rowmanlittlefield.com

PO Box 317
Oxford
OX2 9RU, UK

British Library Cataloguing in Publication Information Available

Library of Congress Cataloging-in-Publication Data

Lewis, Hal M.
  From Sanctuary to Boardroom : a Jewish approach to leadership / Hal M. Lewis.
    p. cm.
  Includes bibliographical references and index.
  ISBN-13: 978-0-7425-5228-9 (cloth : alk. paper)
  ISBN-10: 0-7425-5228-4 (cloth : alk. paper)
  ISBN-13: 978-0-7425-5229-6 (pbk. : alk. paper)
  ISBN-10: 0-7425-5229-2 (pbk. : alk. paper)
  1. Jewish leadership—United States. 2. Leadership—Religious
aspects—Judaism. 3. Jews—United States—Politics and government—21st
century. 4. Jews—United States—Social life and customs—21st century.
5. Synagogues—United States—Administration and organization. 6. Synagogue
trustees—United States. I. Title.

E184.355.L48 2006
296.6'1—dc22   2006009731

Printed in the United States of America

∞ ™ The paper used in this publication meets the minimum requirements of American
National Standard for Information Sciences—Permanence of Paper for Printed Library
Materials, ANSI/NISO Z39.48-1992.

For my mother, of blessed memory,
whose influence remains with me always

Contents

Acknowledgments

My interest in Judaism and leadership first took root around the kitchen table of my parents' home. Those early discussions stimulated a lifelong passion for the issues explored in this book. Though my mother died just as I began to write the manuscript, her guiding influence remains palpable in so many ways. Thankfully, my father continues as a steady source of inspiration to his entire family, daily embodying the courage and strength of which so many effective leaders are made.

In my professional and academic work, I have been privileged to know and learn from many who toil as volunteers and professionals in the vineyards of God, Torah, and the Jewish people. Dedicated and committed individuals all, I trust that they, their colleagues, and those who follow them will use this work to derive meaning and insight from Judaism's enduring lessons on effective leadership.

In the course of writing this book, I have benefited immeasurably from the thoughtful comments, and occasional critique, of trusted colleagues and friends. My gratitude to all who have helped in this regard and in particular to Dr. Dean Bell, Janet Elam, Mark Kurtz, Merritt Mulman, and, most especially, my brother, Paul.

To the administration of the Spertus Institute of Jewish Studies and to Mrs. Jacob S. Cohn, my sincere thanks and appreciation for their support of this project.

My extended family and friends have encouraged me throughout this process, and I thank them profusely.

Happily, my wonderful children, Benjamin and Rachel, have each chosen to pursue exciting paths of leadership of their own. May they always feel comfortable plumbing the depths of our tradition for guidance and inspiration.

My wife, Mary, has supported me through every stage of this book. She is living proof that leadership assumes many forms and manifests itself in a variety of contexts. I am grateful to her beyond words.

Introduction

In every corner of contemporary American society, calls for strong leadership seem to be ubiquitous. In companies and civic institutions, political entities, charitable organizations, even sports franchises, the refrain is the same, "what we need is great leadership." Every problem in the world today, large and small, seems to be framed in terms of a crisis in leadership. When businesses collapse amidst scandal or unanticipated volatility, the reason is cast as a failure of leadership. When athletic teams lose, it is the coach who must be replaced. When political parties fail to meet electoral expectations, it is time to change leadership. Even in religious institutions, it is the spiritual leader who is believed responsible for the well-being of his or her congregants.

The contemporary American Jewish community is certainly no exception. In the United States today there are literally thousands of Jewish organizations, agencies, and institutions. They range from synagogues to cultural groups, and include Jewish Community Centers (JCCs), federations, and educational enterprises, among many, many others. They represent an enormous diversity of ideology, mission, history, size, geographic focus, and operating style. Their funding and constituencies are often widely disparate. Yet, despite these differences, American Jewish organizations seem to share an overarching concern for the future of their leadership. Issues include where will the next generation of Jewish leaders come from, who will train them, and what skills will they require to excel in the years ahead. Responding to this crisis in leadership has caused growing concern across the breadth of American Jewry.[1]

This book is about Jewish leadership. It is designed to provide those who serve (or may someday serve) the Jewish community with an understanding of what it means to be an authentic Jewish leader, as well as pragmatic insights into how to lead effectively from a Jewish perspective. It is written for volunteers and professionals and rabbis and laypeople. It attempts to answer a number of relevant questions for those who see themselves, or are seen by others, as Jewish communal leaders. How does one become a Jewish leader? What are the skills, attributes, and behaviors necessary to lead effectively? How important is leadership to the success of a Jewish community? And, to what degree are today's Jewish leaders different from those of earlier epochs? At the same time, it raises a number of questions that many would likely prefer remain unasked. In what sense are the heads of today's Jewish organizations leaders or merely holders of titled positions? What should the role of wealth and learning be in Jewish communal leadership? Why is it that after expending enormous amounts of money and energy on leadership training and development, many are still asking, "Where have all the great Jewish leaders gone?" And finally, can one speak of Jewish communal leaders at all anymore, given that increasing numbers of American Jews have chosen to disassociate themselves from the organized community in record numbers?[2]

At its core, this book is predicated on the overarching assumption that Judaism, as refracted through the prism of premodern classical texts, contains a great deal of valuable and practical insights into leadership—insights that can help to improve the quality of one's leadership and thereby reduce the crises currently plaguing American Jewish institutions. Though neither a textbook nor a how-to manual, this work will introduce the reader to a variety of these ancient sources in an effort to understand and apply them to the realities faced by contemporary Jewish leaders in their daily work.

Because this book involves the study of classical Jewish teachings on leadership and is not a survey of notable personalities or famous Jewish leaders of bygone eras, reading it is not intended to be a passive experience. Indeed, any serious encounter with traditional Jewish sources demands that the reader engage with the texts in highly personal ways. The issues addressed by this material are challenging and require considerable self-awareness and candid reflection. Readers will be impelled to evaluate their own leadership in light of the principles discussed. More often than not, these texts will become clear only after multiple readings and prolonged discussion with others— colleagues, teachers, critics, and followers.

As they wend their way through the chapters in this book, some may yearn for a simpler approach. After all, this is an era in which complex issues are routinely reduced to succinct bullet points, and books calling themselves "something *for Dummies*" are commonplace. Those who take both Judaism and leadership seriously, however, will come to see that there is nothing simple about either. It is for them that this book was written.

Sadly, much of the wisdom on leadership found in Jewish sources is largely unknown to the very women and men who work on behalf of the Jewish community. As a result, not only have they *not* incorporated Jewish teachings into their own personal and organizational leadership efforts, but most have become convinced that the only worthwhile insights into effective leadership derive from secular sources. Consequently, rather than plumbing the depths of their own tradition, today's Jewish leaders routinely seek leadership expertise from business schools, organizational development groups, and consulting firms. Thus, at precisely the time when so many have returned to Judaism for its wisdom on spirituality, mysticism, and theology, American Jewry's leaders have turned elsewhere for insights into leadership.

Adding to the irony of this situation in which so-called Jewish leaders embrace the leadership insights of non-Jewish sources, while remaining largely ignorant of their own, is the fact that, with increasing frequency, ancient Jewish precepts are today being corroborated by the most rigorously researched and highly regarded findings on effective leadership from the academic and business arenas. Thus, unlike the leadership ephemera often embraced by today's Jewish organizational heads, premodern Jewish insights continue to retain their resonance and timelessness.

Since so much of this book is predicated upon Judaism's classical literature, a few additional observations about the sources to be studied are in order. The material presented comes from a variety of works and spans a vast historical continuum, beginning with the Bible and extending, in some cases, to the modern period. Some of it is legalistic in nature, reflecting laws from the Torah and rabbinic literature, medieval responsa, codes, and enactments, as well as subsequent legal opinions from a variety of halakhic authorities. Other sources are taken from Judaism's extralegal literature, the midrashic tradition, including biblical commentaries, rabbinic interpretations, kabbalistic writings, hasidic tales, and related material. On occasion, ethical treatises, liturgical compositions, communal records, and philosophical discourses will also be included. Not surprisingly, given the wide expanse from which this material is drawn, the sources do not always agree with each other. In view of the fact that they were written by different people at different times, in a diversity of locales, they quite naturally reflect divergent concepts, understandings, formats, and biases. When sources do conflict, no attempt is made to obfuscate the differences between them or to arbitrarily fabricate a single "Jewish" approach to leadership. Rather, readers will be encouraged to consider each perspective in its own context, and to draw conclusions as to the applicability and appositeness of its teachings, based on personal experiences in the contemporary Jewish community.

In spite of their manifold differences, however, it will become clear that these texts share at least three things in common. First, an overwhelming number of them are unapologetically theological in nature. They reflect Judaism's basic contention that human leadership can only be understood in the context of a relationship with God. While today's Jewish communal officials need not share that view, they must, at a minimum, be willing to understand the *Weltanschauung* of their predecessors.

Secondly, even when texts come from divergent historical periods, their authors frequently assume an unbroken, continual chain of connectivity amongst and between them that is very much panepochal. There is a certain intertextuality to these sources that defies conventional understandings of chronology. Thus, it is not uncommon for an author writing in one country at one point in time to respond to the arguments and hermeneutics of a precursor living centuries earlier in a completely different venue, as if they were contemporaries.

Finally, regardless of the date and place of composition, many of these sources presuppose their author's first-hand familiarity with a number of seminal events, despite the fact that, in actuality, few, if any, of them ever experienced these episodes personally. Judaism's proclivity to "see the past in the present tense" and to act as if all Jews, regardless of birthdates, "share" the experience of having been together at certain pivotal milestones, are critical to understanding these sources on leadership. Among those premodern "shared" landmarks which provide the basis for so much of Judaism's approach to leadership are the Egyptian enslavement, the revelation at Sinai, the conquest of the land of Israel, the establishment and subsequent dissolution of the Israelite monarchy, the Babylonian exile, and life in the self-governing *kehillot* (local Jewish communities) of medieval Europe. So, for example, having "lived through" the disastrous experience with monarchy in the biblical period, Don Isaac Abravanel (1437–1508), a Sephardic exegete actually living in fifteenth- and sixteenth-century Europe, could call upon those experiences in helping him craft a remarkably sophisticated leadership model in his own time. By the same token, twenty-first-century American rabbis explain their authority to lead by referencing a process first described in the Torah, known as *semikhah*—ordination.[3] Thus, today's Jewish spiritual leaders, who frequently have more in common with their Christian colleagues than the biblical prophets and ancient sages, nevertheless conceive of their own leadership as if Moses, himself, had laid his hands directly upon them, as he did Joshua and the seventy elders.[4]

Before leaving the topic of texts and source material, a word of explanation about language is appropriate. Some readers will be troubled by the lack of gender neutrality in the translations (and occasionally in the narrative) when reference is made to God. Most often this manifests itself in the use of male pronouns—Him, His, Himself. The decision to utilize what some consider antiquated language was made for stylistic, not theological reasons only. It derives from the firm conviction that phrases such as "God Godself" or "God wants God's children . . ." instead of "God Himself" and "God wants His children" are too awkward and distracting to serve a greater good. While far from a theosophical expert, the author summarily rejects the view that God is a sexual being in any anthropomorphic sense. Use of male pronouns, then, is simply a judgment call regarding a preferred linguistic style. Readers wishing to use these texts but who are, in fact, troubled by this decision should feel free to interpolate or modify accordingly.

In an effort to provide the broadest context in which to understand and apply Judaism's insights on leadership, this book combines (1) a theoretical presentation of the relevant textual material; (2) consideration of how these precepts compare to some of the general literature on leadership; and (3) selected thoughts, honed from more than three decades of Jewish communal service, on current practices in the Jewish community in light of these teachings. In the first four chapters, Judaism's classical approaches to the foundations of leadership are explored. Chapter 1, "A Nuanced Approach," looks at the place of leadership in community and examines the often ambivalent attitude toward leaders found in Jewish sources. Chapter 2, "Authorizing Power," investigates where a leader's power comes from and how traditional sources of authority and legitimacy have evolved and developed over time. Ancient and modern attempts to circumscribe the powers of Jewish leaders are presented in chapter 3, "Limiting Power." Chapter 4, "Power-Sharing," discusses Judaism's tripartite approach to effective communal leadership.

The next three chapters look at Judaism's teachings on what constitute the most efficacious approaches to leadership. Chapter 5, "Beyond the Great Man," considers the consequences for leaders when the pretext of perfection is removed from their work. Chapter 6, "Of Competence and Character," raises a number of questions relative to what leaders are required to know and do, the importance of ethics and integrity to a leader's overall success, and the role of wealth in Jewish communal leadership, among others. As its title suggests, chapter 7, "The Behaviors of Effective Leaders," analyzes a set of six behaviors that Jewish sources have consistently identified as key to successful leadership over the millennia. In chapter 8, "Jewish Leadership for the Twenty-first Century," a vision of authentic and effective Jewish leadership in a radically changing American Jewish community is suggested. A brief summary chapter, "A Final Reflection," concludes the work.

As a book about Judaism and leadership, it is hoped that these pages will speak with particular poignancy to those who serve the Jewish community. At the same time, however, Judaism's insights on leadership have application far beyond the confines of the organized Jewish world. Indeed, they resonate often with an unanticipated profundity, deep into the putatively secular realms of business, politics, communal affairs, and interpersonal relations. Consequently, while the chapters that follow focus unapologetically upon the needs of the American Jewish communal infrastructure and those who lead it, it is possible, and perhaps desirable, that the journey about to commence will extend far beyond the Jewish community.

NOTES

1. See my article, "Making Leaders: How the American Jewish Community Prepares Its Lay Leaders," *Journal of Jewish Communal Service* 80, no. 2–3 (Summer/Fall 2004): 151–59.

2. Steven M. Cohen and Arnold M. Eisen, *The Jew Within* (Bloomington: Indiana University Press, 2000).

3. Numbers 11:16–17; 27:22–23; Deuteronomy 34:9.

4. Also see *Avot* 1:1.

Chapter One

A Nuanced Approach

In a world that generally views leadership as the single most important factor in the success of an enterprise, it may come as something of a surprise to know that the Bible (*Tanakh*) and later Jewish sources reflect an attitude of considerable ambivalence toward human leadership. On the one hand, Judaism recognizes that all societies and organizations require leaders, and that leadership is not only necessary, but can, in fact, be enormously helpful. On several occasions, the Book of Judges, for example, makes it clear that without a strong leader, normal human behavior, left to its own devices, runs the risk of degenerating into nihilism. "In those days there was no king in Israel; every man did that which was right in his own eyes."[1] A similar idea is conveyed in even more graphic terms when the Mishnah instructs, "Pray for the welfare of the government, for were it not for the fear of it, people would swallow each other alive."[2] The great ninth- and tenth-century Jewish philosopher, Saadia Gaon (882–942), expanded these concepts and cast an even more appreciative light upon the benefits of leadership.

> . . . the highest object of human striving in this world ought to be eminence, majesty, and the occupation of a position of leadership . . . were it not for this aspiration toward leadership, there would have been no means of keeping the world in order or of looking after its welfare. It is thanks to its authority that kings are able to conduct wars and take charge of their countries' defense, that judges can judge among law-abiding men and the overseers correct the incorrigible among them.[3]

With consistency, wherever Jews lived across the millennia, their writings reflected similar sentiments.

On the other hand, Judaism has always been more than a little ill at ease with the idea of strong leaders. While one might assume that this derives from centuries of oppressive rule by outsiders, in fact, Judaism's suspicion of leadership applies equally to Jewish leaders as well. Emblematic of this wariness

7

is the charge leveled against Moses himself early in his career, as he sought to bring a sense of order, safety, and security to his enslaved coreligionists.

> Some time after that, when Moses had grown up, he went out to his kinsfolk and witnessed their labors. He saw an Egyptian beating a Hebrew, one of his kinsmen. He turned this way and that and, seeing no one about, he struck down the Egyptian and hid him in the sand. When he went out the next day, he found two Hebrews fighting; so he said to the offender, "Why do you strike your fellow?" He retorted, "Who made you chief and ruler over us?"[4]

While contemporary Jewish leaders, long accustomed to being questioned by *their* followers, may find solace in knowing that even Moses's leadership was challenged, the reality is that, in the case at hand, Moses's query was neither heavy-handed nor unilateral. His behavior toward the Hebrew slaves could hardly be called autocratic. Yet, the text makes it clear that they resented Moses's arrogation of power and control over them, even if his intentions were noble. As will be seen, these verses from the beginning of Exodus set the tone for much of subsequent Jewish writing on the subject of leadership.

At the core of Judaism's concern is that human leaders often see themselves, or are seen by others, as replacements for God. This theme is introduced most powerfully in the *Tanakh*'s discussion of the rise of monarchy in ancient Israel. The Book of Judges records that Gideon, a precursor to the Israelite kings, was so revered for his military prowess and exceptional diplomacy that the reigning tribal heads beseeched him to establish a permanent dynastic regime over the nation. "Then the men of Israel said to Gideon, 'Rule over us—you, your son, and your grandson as well; for you have saved us from the Midianites.'"[5] While such a structure would have differed materially from the then prevailing system, in which judges governed on an ad hoc basis only, the text gives no indication of any objections being registered to this radically new model of strong, permanent leadership. In fact, Gideon's incomparable status appears more than sufficient to have silenced any potential protest. He, however, would have no part of such a plan, and in his refusal he articulated a fundamental tenet of Judaism's attitude toward leadership. "I will not rule over you myself, nor shall my son rule over you; the Lord alone shall rule over you.'"[6]

Gideon's demurral, however, does not alter the people's desire for a more comprehensive form of leadership. When finally they get their king, there can be no confusion as to the costs.

> All the elders of Israel assembled and came to Samuel at Ramah, and they said to him, "You have grown old, and your sons have not followed your ways. Therefore

appoint a king for us to govern us like all other nations." Samuel was displeased that they said, "Give us a king to govern us." Samuel prayed to the Lord, and the Lord replied to Samuel. "Heed the demand of the people in everything they say to you. For it is not you that they have rejected; *it is Me they have rejected as their king* (emphasis added)."[7]

God's reaction is neither tenebrous nor equivocal. The decision to have a king, while tolerated, is understood to be a blatant rejection of divine sovereignty. As a result, subsequent generations of Jewish authorities will be hard-pressed to ignore the intensity and enduring impact of God's rejoinder.

In fact, this idea, that when human beings assume leadership roles they run the risk of usurping God, is repeated and expanded upon throughout Jewish literature. Isaiah, for example, excoriates those whose faith in the leadership of humans prevents them from trusting in God.

Ha! Those who go down to Egypt for help and rely upon horses! They have put their trust in abundance of chariots, in vast numbers of riders, and they have not turned to the Holy One of Israel, they have not sought the Lord.[8]

The medieval Jewish statesman and philosopher, Don Isaac Abravanel, adds his own distinctive voice to the issue. Belief in the absolute sovereignty of God cannot coexist with the embrace of a human monarch, he argued. "By appointing a king, Israel rejected God, the one and only King."[9] Abravanel's passionate critique of monarchy is made all that more potent by the fact that, as a counselor to rulers across Europe, he had intimate knowledge of his subject.

Given Judaism's insistence upon the absolute sovereignty of God and its corollary contention that human leadership is an encroachment on His rule, it would hardly be surprising if Jewish sources advocated a form of anarchism, a governmental system in which human leaders are considered unnecessary. As indicated, however, this is *not* the case, and a variety of classical sources, beginning with the Torah itself, recognize the indispensability of human leadership. It will be in the reconciling of these seemingly contradictory positions—opposition to human leadership *and* recognition of its necessity—that Judaism's nuanced approach becomes most apparent and where today's leaders will find both inspiration and practical guidance for their work.

Significant progress toward resolving these conflicting views is facilitated by the fact that, while tolerating leaders, traditional sources consciously mitigate their right to rule by insisting that their *authority* comes from God. To be sure, leaders may accede to power in a variety of ways: heredity, election, appointment, and the like, but in the end, as the sages taught, "Even a super-intendent of a well [a relatively minor leadership post] is appointed in heaven."[10]

As seen in an earlier text (I Samuel 8:4–7), the unanimous petition of the heads of Israel would not have been enough to force Samuel's acquiescence in the appointment of a king. It took God's sanction, albeit with considerable reservation, before Samuel proffered his approval. Not only did God autho-rize the institution of kingship in this one case, but subsequently, individual sovereigns would be reminded regularly that God was the ultimate source of their success. In the following selection from Psalms, for example, there can be little doubt as to the provenance of King David's manifold accomplish-ments.

I have found David, My servant; anointed him with My sacred oil. My hand shall be constantly with him, and My arm shall strengthen him. No enemy shall oppress him, no vile man afflict him. I will crush his adversaries before him; I will strike down those who hate him. My faithfulness and steadfast love shall be with him; his horn shall be exalted through My name.[11]

To the talmudic rabbis, this idea that God sanctions leadership applied not only to kings and queens but to all who held leadership posts within the com-munal enterprise.

When Rabbi Haggai appointed community leaders, he would have them carry a Torah scroll, by way of saying that every sort of authority bestowed is bestowed with Torah's authorization, as it is said, "By me kings reign by me rulers rule" (Proverbs 8:15–16).[12]

Curiously, this view that human leaders derive their authority directly from God led Don Isaac Abravanel, whose ardent opposition to monarchy has already been mentioned, to take a position that at first seems counterintuitive on the question of a sovereign's tenure. On those occasions, he argued, when a king oversteps his bounds and violates the law (which Abravanel considered inevitable), the people are, nevertheless, *not* permitted to overthrow him because, "God brought kings to power, and only He can depose them."[13]

The concept that leaders, even secular leaders, must look to God as the source of their ultimate authority, is also reflected in the liturgy recited in many contemporary synagogues. While the exact wording may differ from congregation to congregation, the following "Prayer For Our Country" ech-oes a now familiar theme:

Our God and God of our ancestors: We ask Your blessings for our country, for its government, for its leader and advisors, and for all who exercise just and rightful authority. Teach them insights of Your Torah, that they may administer all affairs of state fairly, that peace and security, happiness and prosperity, justice and freedom may forever abide in our midst.[14]

Importantly, this prayer does not ask that leaders heed the will of the people but rather that they remain forever cognizant of, and beholden to God as the ultimate source of all leadership.

In the aggregate then, it is not an exaggeration to suggest that classical Jewish sources see human leadership as something of a concession or compromise. When it comes to leadership, God alone is the Ideal Leader. Human beings must never be allowed to accrue so much power that they displace the divine, nor may they behave as if leadership is their inherent right. Subsequent chapters will explore how Jewish authorities and communities throughout the ages responded to these precepts by seeking to simultaneously authorize and circumscribe the powers of human leaders.

Considering Judaism's view that leadership is a capitulation of sorts, and something far from idyllic, it is not surprising that Jewish sources frequently assume a highly cautious, even distrustful, posture toward those in high positions. This is particularly true of the writings known as *Pirkei Avot* (*Chapters of the Sages*). A tractate of the *Mishnah*, redacted in the early third century CE in the land of Israel, its style is more aphoristic than narrative or discursive. *Pirkei Avot* reflects many of the concerns the ancient rabbinical sages had about power and governance. "Shemayah said, 'Love work; hate lordship; and seek no intimacy with the ruling power.'"[15] Even more sobering is the admonition of Rabban Gamliel:

> Be cautious with the ruling authorities, for they befriend a person only for their own needs. They appear as friends when it is to their advantage, but they do not stand by the individual at the time of that person's distress.[16]

In light of these concerns, not only is leadership at best a dubious compromise, but even prominent leaders are perennially imperfect and untrustworthy. It seems hard to envision, then, that Jewish sources would adopt anything more than a begrudging attitude toward those who hold office. Once again, however, Judaism's nuanced approach to leadership militates against drawing such overly facile conclusions. In fact, for all of its reservations about leaders, Jewish tradition insists that they occupy a unique and treasured place in the world. In the case of the ancient Israelite monarchs, for example, whatever initial resistance there may have been, God eventually makes it clear that He is intimately involved in their identification and selection. Indeed, long before the concepts of personal messiah (*mashiah*) or the messianic age (*y'mot ha'mashiah*) enter the Jewish lexicon, the kings of Israel are referred to as "*meshiah YHWH*," the anointed ones of God, Himself.[17]

Similarly, the rabbis of the Talmud said that not only does God sanction leadership, in general, but He "*personally*" selects all those who lead. "There are three things which the Holy One, blessed be He, Himself proclaims, namely famine, plenty, and a good leader."[18] As verification of this "fact," the sages cite a proof text from the Torah that reads, "See I have called by name Bezalel, the son of Uri."[19] The reference here is to God's naming the artisan, Bezalel, as the one to oversee construction of the desert tabernacle. To the rabbis, the phrase "I have called by name . . ." confirms that God does, indeed, get involved directly in choosing leaders. By extension, the very process of divine selection assures a special and enduring relationship between those who lead and God. Thus, as the case of Bezalel proves, not only is there a unique bond between the Holy One and the handful of people who would become kings and queens, but even leaders whose sphere of influence is considerably more modest are esteemed by the divine.

Moreover, according to both the Torah and later talmudic sources, leaders are entitled to a level of respect normally reserved only for God. "You shall not curse God, nor curse a ruler of your people," the Torah commands, without making a distinction between the two.[20] In their commentaries on the Book of Exodus, the rabbis argued that when the Israelites angrily spoke out against Moses, following their departure from Egypt, they were, in fact, criticizing God directly.[21] Precisely because God selected Moses, as He does all leaders, chastising him was tantamount to disparaging the Holy One, Himself.

Arguably, all of this makes sense when the referent is Moses or even kings, queens, and tabernacle designers. But, what of more ordinary types? Or worse, what about leaders with obvious flaws? Is such regard due them as well? In a fascinating talmudic text the rabbis argue that the *Tanakh* does, indeed, insist that *all* who lead are to be highly valued.

> Scripture says, "And Samuel said to the people, 'It is the Lord that appointed Moses and Aaron'" (I Samuel 12:6) and [in the same passage]: "And the Lord sent Jerubaal and Bedan (Samson), and Jephthah and Samuel" (I Samuel 12:11). Thus Scripture places three less-worthy leaders on the same level as three of Israel's most estimable leaders, to teach you that in his generation Jerubaal is to be considered as Moses was in his generation; Bedan (Samson) in his generation is to be considered as Aaron was in his generation; Jephthah in his generation is to be considered as Samuel was in his generation. To teach you also that *the least worthy, once appointed leader of a community, is to be esteemed as the most eminent among the eminent* (emphasis added).[22]

Embedded within these clever juxtapositions is a critical idea, namely, in a tradition which holds that God Himself is involved in the process of selecting and sanctioning leaders, even those who lack the gravitas of their predecessors must still be treated with deference and honor.

This text seems to have a particularly poignant message for many in today's Jewish world. Given the popular proclivity to refuse leadership positions on the professed basis that one is not "up to" the task, or that one's abilities pale in comparison to communal leaders of bygone eras, these words provide a thoughtful antidote. One ought not recuse himself or herself from accepting leadership in the community on the basis of such faulty comparisons. Leadership is, by definition, always a flawed endeavor. Even so, God extends His sanction to leaders in each generation, and the people must do the same. Individuals who hide behind their purported unworthiness are deceiving themselves, their communities, and God.

Further support for this idea comes from the words of the sage, Rabbi Assi:

> When Rabbi Assi was dying, his nephew saw him weeping. He said: "Why do you weep? Is there any part of the Law which you have not learnt? Your disciples sit before you. Is there any deed of loving kindness which you have not done? And over and above all these qualities, you have kept yourself far from the judge's office, and you have not brought it over yourself to be appointed as an official for the needs of the community." He replied, "That is why I weep. Perhaps I shall have to give an account [i.e., to be condemned] because I was able to be a judge and did not judge. A man who retires to his house and says, 'What have I to do with the burden of the community, or with their suits,' why should I listen to their voice? Peace to thee, O my soul—such a one destroys the world."[23]

Even if Rabbi Assi's words are excessively hyperbolic (an entirely forgivable sin under the circumstances), his message is clear. Societies, organizations, and institutions—all need leaders. When those who can serve decline to do so, they risk jeopardizing much more than just their own futures.

Contemporary readers of these ancient texts cannot help but be struck by their insights and potential applicability. The pragmatism of these classical teachings is all the more remarkable in view of the Bible's initial qualms. This is true not only in sources that consider the theoretical aspects of leadership, but also in those that reflect upon the day-to-day experiences of what it means to be a leader.

Ironic as it may seem, the same classical tradition that urges extreme caution around leaders manifests considerable compassion and concern for their plights as individuals. Premodern Jewish sources knew what every contemporary Jewish leader also understands—being a leader can be both exhilarating and exhausting. High office comes with ample benefits and significant risks.

Being an effective leader often means sacrificing personal comforts, from precious sleep to quality family time. Commenting on the verse that describes Moses's activity on the eve of the revelation at Mt. Sinai: "And Moses went down from the mount to the people" (Exodus 19:14), the rabbis note the following: "Moses did not turn to his own affairs, did not even go down to his house, but went directly 'from the mount to the people.'"[24] Moses's example of self-sacrifice has become a model for subsequent Jewish leaders. Rabbi Judah ha-Nasi, the head of the community in late-second and early-third-century CE Palestine, reportedly observed that leaders who are "busy attending to the needs of the people [are] not even allowed to sleep."[25]

An intriguing text reveals just how much the rabbis understood about the potential personal costs of leadership. Envisioning a mythical conversation between Moses's sister, Miriam, and his wife, Zipporah, the rabbis acknowledge the enormous toll leadership takes on one's family life. In the scenario they construct, Miriam speculates about the exuberant pride that spouses of newly appointed communal leaders must feel. "Miriam said, '[How] happy these men's wives must be at what they see—how their husbands have risen to authority.'" Far from concurring, Zipporah, the experienced and wise spouse of the archetypal Jewish communal leader, retorts without hesitation, "Alas for these wives."[26]

Beyond family issues, leadership often exacts a huge price upon the psyche and emotional state of the individual leader as well. When people move from the private realm to the public arena, they suddenly find themselves exposed, for the first time, to harsh criticisms from their followers. As the great Rabbi Akiva observed, such individuals often go from relative anonymity to "being abused" and even "being regarded as reprehensible."[27] Many contemporary leaders, from national politicos to chief executive officers, are woefully unprepared for this "fishbowl phenomenon." They resist and resent the intrusiveness and unreasonable expectations that seem to come with high office. Jewish communal leaders are no exception. Often motivated by a heartfelt desire to "help out" or to "give back" to the community, they quickly become disillusioned by the intense pressure and omnipresent critiques. Rabbi Akiva's words serve as an appropriate warning for all who are looked upon as leaders. For better or for worse, among the inherent risks of leadership are disparagement, elevated scrutiny, and unwanted public attention.

One of Akiva's most distinguished disciples, Rabbi Nehemiah, described an added risk that challenges today's leaders as well as those of earlier epochs. Notes Nehemiah, when individuals become leaders they suddenly find themselves having to shoulder many more weighty responsibilities. While private citizens can afford to maintain an attitude of relative insouciance regarding the behavior of the community-at-large, those who hold important positions cannot.

> Rabbi Nehemiah said: "As long as one is but an ordinary scholar, he has no concern with the congregation and is not punished [for its lapses], but as soon as he is appointed head and dons the cloak of leadership, he must no longer say: 'I live for my own benefit, I care not about the congregation,' but the whole burden of the community is on his shoulders. If he sees a man causing suffering to another, or transgressing, and does not prevent him, then he is held punishable."[28]

Rabbi Nehemiah's words demand to be taken seriously. Judaism insists upon accountability from its leaders. As the head of any enterprise, a leader's sphere of responsibility extends far beyond his or her personal behavior. Only those prepared to carry the burdens of the larger organization will succeed as leaders.

Painful as it is to contemplate, sometimes the price of leadership is even more costly. In fact, several rabbinic sources indicate that, in the extreme, leadership contributes to premature death. According to Rabbi Judah, one of the three things in this world known to "shorten a person's days" is becoming a public leader.[29] Rabbi Johanan offered a similar perspective when he taught, "Woe to authority which buries its possessor . . ."[30] Rabbi Eleazar ben Azariah, among the youngest people ever to be appointed *nasi*, head of the Jewish community in ancient Palestine, was apparently an exception that proved this rule. Remarking upon the unusual fact that he lived a full life of leadership, the rabbis of the Jerusalem Talmud relate the following:

> Rabbi Eleazar ben Azariah said, "I am some seventy years old." Though he had attained authority, he nevertheless lived long. Thus you learn that authority generally shortens life.[31]

The wisdom of these classical Jewish sources is borne out repeatedly in a variety of modern settings. In a recently published sweeping study of rulers who came to power within the past one hundred years, the eminent University of Kentucky psychiatry professor, Arnold Ludwig, delineates a long and frightening list of dangers associated with leadership. Significantly, his research comes not from the "primitive" premodern era but from the twentieth century. Included among the major hazards of leadership are accelerated aging, an array of mental and physical illnesses, exile, imprisonment, torture, and assassination or execution. Concludes Dr. Ludwig:

> Being a ruler is one of the most lethal activities known to mankind. To my knowledge, there is not another profession pursued over an average ten-year period that is

even close in potential dangerousness. The only nonprofessional activity I am aware of that has a comparable mortality rate is playing Russian roulette with a five-chamber gun about once a year.[32]

While, to be sure, perils vary considerably across a wide continuum of leadership types, the reality remains, as Judaism's classical sources make clear, leadership is an inordinately risky business. Why then, would anyone pursue, or even accept, such tasks? Here again, Jewish sources reveal themselves to be enormously insightful. For all of its dangers, they suggest, leadership can be both rewarding and enlivening.

The rabbis understood that, for many, high office brings tangible personal payoffs. Rather than paint an unrealistic picture, in which the benefits of leadership appear in only lofty, noble, and idealistic hues, the Talmud says, "As soon as a man is appointed leader of a community, he becomes rich."[33] In addition to frequently providing an array of pecuniary advantages, networking opportunities, and business contacts, positions of prominence offer individuals a sense of ego gratification, honor, accomplishment, and legitimacy that are difficult to come by through other means. The sages opine that leadership, in spite of its known health risks, not only enhances the quality of life but may even prolong the duration of one's years. In a *midrash* the rabbis go further, arguing that leadership might even be enough to forestall divine punishment.

> Rabbi Huna observed: If a man has been undone by transgression, he incurs the penalty of death at the hands of heaven. What should he do so as to live? . . . Let him go and get himself appointed a communal leader or an administrator of charity and he will remain alive.[34]

Even if understood as nothing more than metaphor, this text indicates the rabbis knew that leadership is not always about self-sacrifice and helping others. More often than not, leaders derive considerable personal privilege from their work.

These rabbinic insights comport with much of what social scientists have come to know about leadership around the world. While leaders may cite an array of high-minded reasons to explain their behavior, including duty, service, patriotism, and the like, there appears to be a strong social and biological drive toward leadership that trumps all noble rationalizations. Further, as Arnold Ludwig observes, "the rewards that come with ultimate power . . . serve as powerful motivators for would-be rulers to do Nature's bidding."[35] He argues that there are four major "perks of power" that are inherent to human leadership: increased access to sexuality and promiscuity, more offspring, opportunities for greater wealth, and deference and respect from followers.[36] While not every leadership post offers equal access to every perk and while not everyone aspires to high office to reap benefits of this sort, Ludwig's research makes it clear, as the ancient Jewish sages recognized long ago, that rank does have its privileges.

Not only are these perquisites of leadership utilitarian in many cases, they are also extraordinarily intoxicating, as well. Once ensconced in such a life, leaders or former leaders find it extremely difficult to simply walk away. Even when people's initial inclination is to refuse leadership, they quickly become enticed by its allure and will go to great lengths to protect their domain.

> Rabbi Joshua ben Qivsay said: "All my life I would run away from office. Now that I have entered it, whoever comes to oust me I will come down upon him with this kettle. Just as a kettle scalds and wounds and blackens, so I will come down upon him."[37]

The Babylonian Talmud reflects the same idea, taught in the name of Rabbi Joshua ben Perahiah, who was himself an experienced leader, having held the title *nasi* (head of the court in Palestine):

> At first whomever were to say to me "Take up the honor" [of leading] I would bind him and put him in front of a lion, but now whomever were to say to me, "Give up the honor," I would pour a kettle of boiling water over him.[38]

On numerous occasions, the *midrashim* echo similar sentiments, including the pithy aphorism, "It is easy to go up to a dais, tough to come down."[39] Even Moses, according to rabbinic folklore, had trouble surrendering power to Joshua, despite the fact that he was the one who insisted on naming a successor in the first place.

> Rabbi Huna said: As soon as God said to Moses, "Hand over your office to Joshua," immediately Moses began to pray to be permitted to enter the land. He can be compared to a governor who so long as he retained his office could be sure that whatever orders he gave, the king would confirm . . . But as soon as he retired and another was appointed in his place, he had in vain to ask the gate-keeper to let him enter [the palace].[40]

Observers of the contemporary scene will immediately recognize the truth in these rabbinic perspectives. All too often—in business, politics, and nonprofit organizational life—established leaders find it difficult, if not impossible, to relinquish power and its manifold trappings. This is particularly common in the case of "founders," those individuals credited with starting the enterprise, or those whose tenures have extended so long that they and their organization are often thought of as one and the same. Because they are unable to envision anyone else at the top, they often resist—sometimes passively, other times, actively—all efforts to transfer the mantle of leadership. In a subsequent chapter consideration will be given to how Judaism views the issues of leadership development and succession of power. At this point, it is sufficient to note, yet again, the profound insight of these ancient sources into the nuances and complexities of leadership.

Recognizing how easy it is to become habituated to the trappings of office led Jewish authorities to caution against the abuses of power. In sharp contrast to the conventional stereotyped leader whose very persona exudes dominance, command, and control, Judaism condemns those leaders who flaunt their station and privilege. Such leaders disappoint God, to the point of tears, according to the rabbis. "Over three the Holy One, blessed be He, weeps every day: over him who is able to occupy himself with the Torah [study] and does not; and over him who is unable to occupy himself with the Torah [study] and does; and over a leader who domineers over the community."[41]

Leaders who "flex their muscles" for no reason other than to show off and assert themselves are counted among the most despicable of all people. They rule by "terror" and, as such, are considered "sinners of Israel." A leader who abuses the privileges of office will be doomed to a life of ignominy—at least as the rabbis understood it. "Any communal leader who makes himself unduly feared by the community . . . will never have a scholar for a son."[42]

As if to underscore the importance of a leader never exploiting the trappings of rank, the rabbis record that when Samson, a former judge known in later life for bravery and heroism in battle, beseeched God, he described himself as follows: "Sovereign of the universe, remember on my behalf that twenty years I judged Israel, and never did I order anyone to carry my staff from one place to another."[43] The point is, of course, that even though Samson might have been forgiven his attempts to capitalize on position and reputation, such behavior is antithetical to good leadership. Acting like a bully and gloating over one's status are as unacceptable as they are commonplace among leaders.

In his medieval legal compendium, the *Mishneh Torah*, Moses Maimonides (1135–1204) codified the underlying principles in these teachings, giving them the formal status of law. "It is forbidden to lead the community in a domineering and arrogant manner . . . [It] is also forbidden to treat the people with disrespect [even if] they be ignorant."[44]

The careful reader will observe that, to this point, very little distinction has been noted between leadership and "authority," that is, official position. A presumption has been made by the authors of the sources studied that the tradition's insights into leadership are germane for *all* who hold titled positions within the community, whether or not they meet some empirical, objective test of true leadership. Regardless of skill sets, competencies, personality, or attributes, the sources seem to suggest that *any* individual recognized as a leader, is, in fact, a leader, subject to the teachings, precepts, and injunctions on leadership. In most of these sources, and, of course, in popular usage (as described in the Introduction), both within and beyond the Jewish community, the word leadership is often used as a synonym for authority.

While there are several reasons to support such an approach, it is not the only way to understand the concept of leadership. In fact, several well-known theorists argue that despite the prevailing tendency to conflate them, it is imperative that sharp distinctions be made between leadership and position. For example, in one of the most creative contemporary studies on effective leadership cowritten by Benjamin Zander, Boston Philharmonic conductor, and his wife, family therapist Rosamund Stone Zander, the authors discuss what they call "leading from any chair." In their groundbreaking work, *The Art of Possibility*, the Zanders argue:

> The conductor of an orchestra does not make a sound. His picture may appear on the cover of the CD in various dramatic poses, but his true power derives from his ability to make other people powerful . . . The activity of leadership is not limited to conductors, presidents, and CEOs . . . the player who energizes the orchestra . . . is exercising leadership of the most profound kind.

"A leader," they conclude, "does not need a podium; she can be sitting quietly on the edge of any chair, listening passionately and with commitment, fully prepared to take up the baton."[45]

Similarly, Harvard University's Ronald Heifetz insists that there are clear differences between leadership and authority. In Heifetz's view, authority refers to the conferral of power upon an individual to perform a service. A rabbi, for example, is hired by a synagogue board for an array of rabbinic functions. Such authority is given and can be taken away; that is, the rabbi can be fired or her contract not renewed. Another example is the election of a popular philanthropist to serve as the president or board chair of the local federation. As a holder of that title, the individual is given authority to govern: to make decisions and to provide answers for an array of technical questions—for example, who should be hired as the executive, how the campaign will run, what speakers to invite for the community dinner, and so forth. This, however, argues Heifetz, is not leadership. For that, an individual must be engaged in helping others to change and to find adaptive solutions to difficult problems over time. Leadership is not governance; it is not about quick fixes, he argues. Nor does it have anything to do with rank, office, or position. On the contrary, those things are related to authority, and while authorities *may* lead, they don't always. For both Heifetz and the Zanders, one need not have authority in order to lead. In fact, authority can often be an impediment to effective leadership, particularly when creativity and enthusiasm give way to bureaucracy and organizational minutiae.[46]

On this debate between those who insist on a strict bifurcation between leadership and authority and those who prefer to call every authority a leader, Judaism prefers a more centrist position. To be sure, classical texts concur with Heifetz and the Zanders that leadership is not always the same as authority. In point of fact, one can often be more effective without title than with it. This idea is reflected in the rabbinic instruction, "Be a tail among lions rather than a head among foxes."[47] In addition, the Hebrew language, itself, conveys a similar message. The word for leader is *manhig* (מנהיג). It derives from a three-letter root, *nun-hey-gimel* (נ-ה-נ), meaning behavior. This root is shared by several other Hebrew words, including *minhag* (מנהג)—practice—and *nahag* (נהג)—driver. Thus, even the Hebrew word itself indicates that leadership is about behavior and activity—not title, station, or office.

On the other hand, Jewish sources clearly indicate that both in common parlance, and in fact, those who hold office *are* looked upon as leaders and are to be treated as such, whether or not they engage their followers in adaptive change. This is certainly the message of the previously examined section of the Talmud from the tractate of *Rosh Hashannah*: "Jephthah [one of the most sinful of the judges] in his generation is to be considered as Samuel [perhaps the greatest judge] was in his generation." Thus, once again, there is evidence that Judaism appreciates the nuances. Certainly, leadership is about more than mere authority. At the same time, however, when the community does extend its authority, those to whom it has been given become its leaders. Therefore, while not every leader needs to have authority (office, position, rank), every recognized communal authority is to be considered a leader.

This pragmatic approach suggests a very important perspective regarding the question of who is eligible to lead, and what, if any, training is required for leaders. In the general literature on leadership the debate over whether leaders are made or born is fabled.[48] While early general theories in the study of leadership reflect the influence of Plato's philosopher-king model in which only certain people are believed endowed from birth with the skills necessary for leadership, the field has evolved over the years to the point that few, if any, serious scholars would accept that notion today.[49] Increasingly, contemporary theorists hold that leading is a process that must be learned and refined over a protracted period and that truly effective leaders must be taught how to lead and must keep on learning to maintain their success.[50]

Importantly, no such debate *ever* took place in Jewish sources. With consistency, very few paradigms of Jewish leadership after the biblical period reflect the view that communal leadership is circumscribed by birthright, physiognomy, or innate characteristics of any sort. On the contrary, with increasing frequency, Jewish sources from the rabbinic period forward suggest that leadership can, and must, be learned.

While certain ancient models of Jewish communal leadership were built upon principles of hereditary inheritance, the Torah itself appears to argue against such a restrictive view. In the nineteenth chapter of Exodus, God tells the Jewish people, "You shall be to Me a kingdom of priests and a holy nation."[51] This phrase—"a kingdom of priests"—*mamlekhet kohanim*—is a curious and powerful one, indeed. Despite the fact that the ancient priesthood was a hereditary and highly exclusive caste, not open to all, the Torah instructs that when it comes to leading, *all* Jews are priests (*kohanim*), and therefore eligible to lead, regardless of lineage or traits, skill sets or intellect. Arguably then, the Torah is laying the groundwork for a far more expansive approach to community leadership than existed in its own time, a view which contemporary leadership expert, Warren Bennis, embraced when he penned the words, "learning to lead is a lot easier than most of us think . . . because each of us contains the capacity for leadership."[52]

Further evidence that classical Jewish sources reject the idea that leaders are born is found in the tradition's approach to leadership training. Long before today's thinkers concluded that leadership can best be acquired not through birthright but through sophisticated instruction, the authors of the *midrash* said the same thing. In commenting upon the verse in Song of Songs (6:11), "I went down into the garden of nuts," one of the sages, Resh Lakish, observed:

> The nut tree is smooth. Anyone who would climb to its top without considering how to do it is sure to fall to his death, thus taking his punishment from the tree. So, too, he who would exercise authority over a community in Israel without considering how to do it is sure to fall and take his punishment from the hands of the community.[53]

Were leadership the province only of those born to it, the need for such consideration would be superfluous. Precisely because the capacity for leadership resides with the many, not the few, the importance of training becomes paramount.

This chapter has examined Judaism's ambivalent attitude toward leadership. On the one hand, the exercise of human influence and power over others represents a usurpation of the divine role; on the other hand, it is essential to the success of nations and organizations, large and small. Paradoxically, leaders are to be distrusted *and* treated with a maximum of respect. They are entitled to an ample array of privileges, yet they are proscribed from flaunting the very advantages of their office.

At the heart of this nuanced approach is the overarching presupposition that all leaders—religious, secular, political, spiritual—owe their success to God. Thus, Judaism both legitimizes the leadership of human beings and preserves the hegemony of God as the singular absolute leader. In the chapter that follows consideration is given to the processes by which leadership models have been created, expanded, and authenticated across the centuries.

NOTES

1. Judges 17:6, 21:25. Also see Judges 18:1, 19:1.
2. *Avot* 3:2.
3. Saadia Gaon, *The Book of Beliefs and Opinions*, trans. Samuel Rosenblatt (New Haven, CT: Yale University Press, 1948), 387.
4. Exodus 2:11–14.
5. Judges 8:22.
6. Judges 8:23.
7. I Samuel 8:4–7.
8. Isaiah 31:1.
9. Don Isaac Abravanel, *Commentary on I Samuel* 8:4.
10. Bava Batra 91b.
11. Psalms 89:21–26.
12. Jerusalem Talmud *Peah* 8:6.
13. Abravanel, *Commentary on Deuteronomy* 17:14. For more on Abravanel's writings on leadership, see B. Netanyahu, *Don Isaac Abravanel* (Philadelphia: The Jewish Publication Society of America, 1982).
14. "A Prayer For Our Country," *Siddur Sim Shalom* (New York: The Rabbinical Assembly, 1985), 415.
15. *Avot* 1:10.
16. *Avot* 2:3.
17. See I Samuel 24:7; 26:11, and II Samuel 19:22. Also see II Samuel 12:7 and II Kings 9:3–12.
18. *Berakhot* 55a.
19. Exodus 31:1–2.
20. Exodus 22:27.
21. *Mekhilta, Be-shallah*, 7.
22. *Rosh Hashannah* 25a–b.

23. *Tanhuma, Mishpatim*, 2.
24. *Mekhilta Yitro* 6.
25. Ecclesiastes Rabbah 5:11:1.
26. *Yalkut Be'ha'alotekha*, 738.
27. Jerusalem Talmud, *Peah* 8:6.
28. Exodus Rabbah 27:9. Also see *Shabbat* 54b.
29. *Berakhot* 55a.
30. *Pesachim* 87b.
31. Jerusalem Talmud, *Berakhot* 1:6, 1:9.
32. Arnold M. Ludwig, *King of the Mountain* (Lexington: The University Press of Kentucky, 2002), 117.
33. *Yoma* 22b.
34. Leviticus Rabbah 25:1.
35. Ludwig, *King of the Mountain*, 1.
36. Ludwig, *King of the Mountain*, 50–78.
37. Jerusalem Talmud, *Pesachim* 6:1.
38. *Menahot* 109b.
39. *Yalkut, Va'et'hanan* 845.
40. Deuteronomy Rabbah 2:5.
41. *Hagigah* 5b.
42. *Rosh Hashannah* 17a.
43. *Sotah* 10a.
44. Moses Maimonides, *Mishneh Torah, Hilkhot Sanhedrin*, Judges 25:1–2.
45. Rosamund Stone Zander and Benjamin Zander, *The Art of Possibility* (Boston: Harvard Business School Press, 2000), 68, 73, 76.
46. Ronald Heifetz, *Leadership Without Easy Answers* (Cambridge, MA: Harvard University Press, 1994), 49–100.
47. *Avot* 4:20.
48. See, for example, Jay A. Conger, *Learning to Lead: The Art of Transforming Managers into Leaders* (San Francisco: Jossey-Bass, 1992), 14–36.
49. Warren Bennis, *On Becoming a Leader* (New York: Basic Books, 2003), xxv–xxxiii.
50. Warren G. Bennis and Robert J. Thomas, *Geeks and Geezers—How Era, Values, and Defining Moments Shape Leaders* (Boston: Harvard Business School Press, 2002), 1–21.
51. Exodus 19:6.
52. Bennis, *On Becoming a Leader*, xxvii.
53. Song of Songs Rabbah 6:11§1.

Chapter Two

Authorizing Power

While twenty-first-century Jewish communal leaders rarely give much thought to the question of where their powers come from, premodern Jewish leaders were particularly interested in understanding the bases upon which they were authorized to lead. An examination of these issues from earlier epochs will provide today's Jewish communal officers with both a useful context as well as valuable lessons designed to help improve their own leadership work.

The Torah recognizes three overarching paradigms of Jewish leadership—the priest, the prophet, and the king.[1] Each prototype is sanctioned and authorized by God directly, and each is accorded considerable power as part of an extensive set of divinely specified job-related responsibilities.

The priests served as primary cultic experts and sacrificial specialists. In addition, they were empowered to perform a number of derivative duties, including establishing the liturgical calendar, controlling marriage, providing medical advice, judging, and teaching. The priests were selected by God Himself and treasured as no others. "And they shall have no inheritance among their brethren; the Lord is their inheritance, as He spoke to them."[2]

The prophets were the spokesmen of God, charged with transmitting divine instruction to the nation at large. They functioned as social critics and were certified to perform miracles, read oracles, and bestow an array of blessings and curses. They too were selected specifically by God (though usually against their will). In this regard, the experience of Jeremiah is typical:

And the word of the Lord came unto me saying: Before I formed you in the belly I knew you, and before you came forth out of the womb I sanctified you; I have appointed you a prophet unto the nations. Then said I: Ah Lord God! Behold, I cannot speak for I am a child.[3]

The kings of Israel were the political heads of the Jewish nation. They held an elaborate portfolio with duties that ranged from domestic affairs to foreign relations. Authorized to protect the polity from military invasion, they served as the nation's chief jurists as well.[4] Along with prophecy and priesthood, the monarchy also received the full support of God. Not only were individual sovereigns considered His anointed ones, but it was with one of the kings, David, that God chose to establish an eternal dynasty, from whom the Messiah himself would descend.

> The Lord declares to you that He, the Lord, will establish a house for you. When your days are done and you lie with your fathers, I will raise up your offspring after you, one of your own issue, and I will establish his kingship. He shall build a house for My name, and I will establish his royal throne forever. I will be a father to him, and he shall be a son to Me . . . Your house and your kingship shall ever be secure before you; your throne shall be established forever.[5]

While the unilateral endorsement of God might seem more than sufficient to legitimate a leader's status, the Bible requires an additional level of authorization for all three of these leadership types, specifically, the consent of the people. In describing the inauguration of the high priest, for example, the Torah records God's instruction to Moses as follows: "Take Aaron and his sons with him . . . Gather the entire community to the entrance of the Tent of Meeting . . ."[6] This is a rather curious requirement. The high priest was the predominant religious leader of the land, already hand selected directly by God. His leadership was automatic and incontestable. Nevertheless, power of the sort accorded the priest had to be witnessed and supported by the entire congregation of Israel. God's sanction was necessary but not sufficient.

Similarly, when the Israelite kings were installed, the presence of the polity-at-large was required. In the case of David, the text reads: "All the tribes of Israel came to David at Hebron . . . All the elders of Israel came to the king at Hebron, and King David made a pact with them in Hebron before the Lord. And they anointed David king over Israel."[7] A similar requirement marked the start of his grandson, Rehoboam's rule: "Rehoboam went to Shechem, for all Israel had come to Shechem to acclaim him as king."[8] This was the pattern that marked the relationship with all the kings of Israel. "And Jehoiada solemnized the covenant between the Lord, on the one hand, and the king and the people, on the other—as well as between the king and the people—that they should be the people of the Lord."[9] Despite being considered God's anointed ones then, those who would assume the vast powers of the monarchy could not begin their rule without an independent authorization from the rank and file.

In the case of the biblical prophets, the potency of divine election would seem to have been more than enough to obviate the need for any additional authorization. Nonetheless, even for the prophets, acknowledgment and endorsement by followers were critical to their leadership. In his seminal work on prophecy, Abraham Heschel noted that by all logical standards, the prophets never should have had *any* followers. "The striking surprise is that prophets of Israel were tolerated at all by their people. To the patriots, they seemed pernicious; to the pious multitude, blasphemous; to the men of authority, seditious."[10]

Merely claiming to speak in the name of God would not have guaranteed responsive followers. As the case of Elijah on Mount Carmel demonstrates, Israelite prophets needed their powers authorized by the people as well.[11] For this reason, they were obligated to prove themselves by a variety of means, including spectacular miracles, public prognostication, and wonderworking.

Thus, key to the prophet's legitimacy was not merely divine selection but the *attribution* of divine selection by the community.

> Prophetic empowerment is derived . . . from the disposition and the need of the community itself to empower such persons. Prophets are persons with electrical cords attached to their bodies. The question is: Where is the wall outlet located into which they plug themselves in (*sic*)? The outlet is located squarely in the community itself.[12]

These biblical leadership typologies, and the bases upon which their work was authorized, set the standard for future generations of Jewish leaders, even to this day. In Judaism, a leader's powers derive from a combination of direct linkage to God *and* parallel authorization from the people at large. Following the close of the biblical period all who would aspire to Jewish communal leadership endeavored to emulate the model of the priest, prophet, and king by claiming *both* divine sanction and the endorsement of their own generation. This often involved a twofold process in which (1) new forms of communal leadership were recast in the image of the biblical models, thereby establishing God's blessing; and (2) the pressing needs of the day were invoked in order to secure the community's authorization of expanded or new powers.

Repeatedly, for example, Jewish authorities insisted that changed circumstances mandated dramatic expansions of the powers accorded the king. Often these new powers were presented as having derived from the Bible's original description of the monarch's duties. Ironically, most of the texts authorizing these new powers were written long after the demise of Jewish sovereignty, but they offer enormous insights nonetheless.

The writings of Moses Maimonides are a case in point. In the *Mishneh Torah*, he expands considerably upon the powers of the king that appeared in the Bible.

> The king is empowered to put to death anyone who rebels against him . . . It is within the province of the king to levy taxes upon the people for his own needs or for war purposes. He fixes the custom duties, and it is forbidden to evade them. He may issue a decree that whoever dodges them shall be punished either by confiscation of his property or by death . . . All the land he conquers belongs to him. He may give thereof to his servants and warriors as much as he wishes; he may keep thereof for himself as much as he wants . . . He may break through [private property] to make a road for himself, and none may protest against it. No limit can be prescribed for the king's road; he expropriates as much as is needed. He does not have to make detours because someone's vineyard or field [is in his way]. He takes the straight route and attacks the enemy.[13]

Similarly, Menachem Meiri (1249–1316), Talmud scholar from Provence, argued that: "At a time of war, he [the king] can also take the produce of fields and vineyards, if they [the army] have nothing to eat . . . He is also permitted to levy a tax for his needs and for waging his wars . . ."[14] From both of these texts it is clear that neither Maimonides nor Meiri was opposed to increasing a king's powers when circumstances so warranted. Nevertheless, no king could do so indiscriminately or merely by virtue of his position. Rather, the escalation of monarchial clout required specific authorizations linking the new powers to those that God had already approved and to the community's recognition of the exigencies at hand.

An additional example of this process is found in the case of the talmudic sages. For these *rabbis*—a position that never even existed in the biblical world—the need to be linked to a Torah-sanctioned leadership type, already blessed by God, was essential. At the same time, however, they had to secure authorization from their community for powers that had never before been legitimated or even envisaged in prior models of communal leadership.

As they sought to respond to the needs of their coreligionists in an era in which the Temple, God's House, had been destroyed, the sacrificial system was upended, and the people were in exile, these new Jewish leaders affirmed their links to God by positioning themselves squarely in the tradition of Moses and the biblical prophets. Unabashedly, they sought to convince others of their right to continue and expand these earlier traditions. "Moses received the Torah at Sinai and handed it down to Joshua; Joshua to the elders; the elders to the prophets; and the prophets handed it down to the men of the Great Assembly," they insisted.[15]

To solidify this connectivity between themselves and Moses, the sages adapted the (previously discussed) ceremony of *semikhah* (ordination). Here rabbis pass on official certification to new colleagues by mimicking the rite used by Moses, in which he placed—*s-m-kh* (ך-מ-ס)—his hands upon those who would succeed him. Further, because it was so important that they establish this unbroken bond between themselves and Moses, the rabbis revised biblical history and began referring to him as *Moshe rabbenu*—Moses, our rabbi—as if to suggest an uninterrupted chain of continuity between his powers and theirs.

Yet, monikers alone would not suffice. The newly emergent rabbinic class required more than the claim of divine authorization in order to become effective leaders. They sought the direct support of the people as well. In so doing, the rabbinical sages had to make it clear to their would-be followers that they were up to the tasks at hand and capable of responding to the new circumstances thrust upon them. To do so, they declared themselves "old and improved"; that is, they were heirs to a venerated tradition but capable of leading in a world marked by a whole new set of realities.

> Rabbi Abdimi from Haifa said: Since the day when the Temple was destroyed, prophecy has been taken from the prophets and given to the sages . . . Although it has been taken from the prophets, it has not been taken from the sages . . . A sage is even superior to a prophet.[16]

Thus, these new Jewish leaders claimed the right to do what none had done before—teach, interpret, and adjudicate the Torah. As they saw it, an entirely new set of national circumstances left no other choice. The times demanded a dramatically expanded set of powers, for which only they were qualified.

The talmudic literature is replete with examples of the rabbis endeavoring to secure the buy-in and support of the polity for this greatly enhanced mission. In some cases, their methods bore a striking resemblance to the miracle working of their prophetic progenitors;[17] in others, they blazed entirely new territory by legitimating their interpretive powers on "rational" or "intuitive" bases. The well-known story of the oven of Akhnai is an example of these latter attempts. In this elaborate yarn in which the rabbis debate a complicated technical issue of religious purity, they affirm their incontrovertible right to make binding legal (halakhic) decisions in cases not specifically covered by Torah law. Audaciously, they arrogate to themselves the power to issue such rulings even in opposition to what appears to be God's original intentions. Now that the Torah has been given, they contend, the answer is no longer in heaven. Their polemic concludes with the assertion that God Himself rejoices at these new powers, making it absolutely clear that the general population should follow suit.[18]

This dynamic, in which, with proper authorizations, a leader's powers are expanded and reconfigured, is an oft-repeated feature of Jewish history. Post-biblical authorities recognize that the Torah simply does not address all of the leadership functions mandated by changed conditions and circumstances. But, since no human leader has absolute authority, capricious aggrandize-ment of power is unacceptable. Establishment of God's sanction, coupled with communal authorization, remain the keys to the evolving growth and enhancement of Jewish leadership.

As was true in the rabbinic period, the Middle Ages witnessed the creation of several new leadership positions, none of which existed in the Bible. Rooted in the massive demographic, sociological, and religious changes of the epoch, these new communal offices were also understood to be extensions of earlier leadership models, ordained by God, and authorized by the commu-nity and its representatives.

During the medieval period, Jews lacked a central, polity-wide authority. They were diffused across Europe and generally lived in communities under either Christian or Islamic domination. To varying degrees, they were accorded limited self-rule—the rights to appoint their own courts, hire their own professionals, establish their own internal communal policies, and main-tain their own religious and social services—provided they complied with an array of externally imposed legislation, often involving the payment of taxes to the ruling authorities.

Among the new leadership posts that emerged in response to these altered realities was the position known as *parnas* or community trustee. This was a lay position in which a typically affluent, well-connected volunteer, often held in high regard in non-Jewish circles as well, was empowered to share responsibility for assessing and collecting taxes, setting communal policy, overseeing the local infrastructure, as well as governing and hiring communal functionaries. The *parnasim* required neither formal training nor certifica-tion; nor were their positions technically hereditary in nature (although wealth was, and still is, often transmitted from parents to children). In view of the considerable influence these "lay leaders" exerted upon medieval Jewish communities, it bears repeating that this category of leadership did not exist in the Torah itself. Nevertheless, Judaism's system of authorizing new and expanded powers enabled an ancient tradition to respond to current realities.

By contemporary standards, a powerful, affluent laity charged with respon-sibilities for communal governance hardly seems groundbreaking. Even in the Middle Ages, given the importance of generating a continuous tax base and the need to fund a variety of local services within the self-governing Jew-ish community, the linkage between wealth and power is hardly surprising. The mere possession of riches, however, was insufficient to automatically guarantee leadership. Affluent citizens could not simply co-opt power or unilaterally take control of the communal reins. As demonstrated repeatedly, in Judaism, the powers to lead derive from a combination of divine sanction and community authorization, not pecuniary muscle flexing.

The processes by which wealthy trustees were empowered to be Jewish communal leaders are complex and highly technical. The present analysis permits only a brief summary of the salient points. Most importantly, the close affinity between certain functions of the *parnasim* and the biblical kings—tax collection, protection of the community, alliances with foreign governments, and the like—made it natural to see the job of communal trustee as a "modernized" iteration of the monarch, already sanctioned by God. Moreover, the rabbis had previously extended the monarchial function to the exilarch (*resh galuta*) in Babylonia, making empowerment of the *parnas* quite logical and reasonable. In addition, the sages had earlier granted certain powers to nonrabbis, including the ability to serve as judges, adjudicate economic matters, and govern particular aspects of communal life.[19] *Parnasim*, therefore, could comfortably claim a preexisting legitimacy. In the aggregate then, these precedents helped to provide the position of *parnas* with the status of an authentic, divinely sanctioned paradigm of Jewish leadership, despite the fact that such a post lacks biblical roots.

Regarding the all-important authorization of the community, a critical step in that direction was taken when recognized legal scholars of the period analogized the local Jewish community council (*kahal* or *kehillah*) to the ancient *beit din* or rabbinical court. When this happened, lay people were assigned all the powers of the court, including the right of expropriation. Prior to this time, the power to expropriate—that is, to take possession of an individual's funds or property for public good—was the primary province of the rabbinic judges. "The rabbis have [the] power to expropriate [for the benefit of the public]"; literally, "(Anything declared) ownerless (*hefker*) by the court (*beit din*) is ownerless (*hefker*)."[20]

Since the power of expropriation meant that judges were able to set and collect fines and enforce a variety of penalties in both civic and criminal cases, it is easy to see why these powers were essential for those leading a self-governing Jewish community in the Middle Ages. With this authorization, *parnasim* could assess and collect the taxes demanded by Christian or Islamic authorities, and they were able to raise the funds necessary to pay for the variety of Jewish religious, educational, and social services provided by the *kehillah* for its residents.

Because decisions of a rabbinical court were binding and not subject to negotiation and because as legal precedents, they extended far beyond the particular case under consideration, individuals with analogous powers came to occupy a place of uncontested leadership in the life of the Jewish community. *Parnasim* were thus able to make and enforce community policy, whether or not local residents approved every one of their decisions or even supported their becoming communal heads in the first place. Without such an authorization, they would have had no recourse if a co-religionist declined to pay his allotted share of the tax burden. Indeed, absent a standing equivalent to that of a rabbinical court, the lay leadership of a given community would have faced the unhappy prospect of residents paying or not paying taxes based on personal whim and caprice.

Given how important these authorizations were to legitimating the role of the *parnasim*, a more in-depth look at some of them will be instructive. In a rabbinic responsum from Barcelona, Solomon ben Abraham Adret (ca. 1235–1310) was called upon to opine on the issue of authority and a leader's right to make binding decisions. After discussing a number of precedent leadership types, including the Israelite kings, the patriarch (*nasi*) in Palestine, and the exilarch (*resh galuta*) in Babylonia, all of whom had the capacity to compel others to follow their dictates, Adret wrote the following:

> So too the decrees or enactments of the majority of the *kahal* [local self-governing council] regarding the needs of the community. Since the majority enacted it, even against the will of individuals, it is valid . . . For in each and every public, individuals are considered to be under the rule of the many and must pay heed to them in all their affairs. They [the minority] stand to the people of their city as all Israel stands to the high court or the king . . .[21]

A similar idea is expressed by a Turkish rabbi, Elijah Mizrahi (ca. 1450–1526), who argued that "the entire community is considered a court in matters concerning its members." He went on to observe:

> This also applies to the leaders of the city, for all the townspeople recognize their authority in matters related to the improvement of communal life, and they, the townspeople, all rely on them. Thus, it is as if the leaders were explicitly chosen, and all their decisions stand. And although some may object to their decrees and ordinances, it is as if they explicitly gave their consent . . .[22]

Obviously, authorization of this sort is extremely potent. Armed with such powers, lay leaders could tax, fine, punish, and even issue edicts banning residents from participating in the life of the community, known as *herem*.

Having been likened to a *beit din*, *parnasim* were suddenly in a position not only to adjudicate but to legislate for members of their *kehillah* as well.[23] The famous German talmudist, Rabbi Gershom ben Judah (ca. 960–1028) made this perfectly clear in a responsum of his own. In language reminiscent of the Talmud on Jephthah and Samuel (*Rosh Hashannah* 25a-b), he wrote: "Whoever is appointed as leader [*parnas*] of the community is as a prince among princes. Therefore, the decree of the communities is valid and their ruling is binding . . ."[24]

To be sure, it is entirely possible that these authorizations were merely complex legalistic machinations designed to legitimize what had already become common practice, namely affluent individuals exerting great influence upon local Jewish communal policy. After all, the security and vitality of medieval Jewish *kehillot* depended, in large measure, upon these prosperous citizens holding prominent posts. Nevertheless, even if these sources depicted an ideal that was not always matched by the realities of Jewish communal life, their significance should not be minimized. In their diversity and intensity they suggest an enduring lesson, namely that power should never automatically become the purview of the wealthy. By a variety of methods (to be looked at in greater detail in chapter 3), including limiting the terms of those who served on local councils, prohibiting nepotism in communal governance, insisting that edicts of excommunication be issued with rabbinic as well as lay sanction, among several others, Jewish authorities of the period insisted that power not be coerced, taken for granted, or assumed to be an absolute, inherent right of the wealthy.[25] Only when the community extended its sanction to a position already believed to be sanctified by God, could individuals, even the wealthiest among them, rightfully exercise power.

Curiously, classical sources apply a similar standard even to Gentile leaders, over whom, for all practical purposes, Jews had little or no control. Several important sources promulgate the principle that the powers of non-Jewish leaders must also be authorized before their decisions can be followed. As a practical matter, of course, this is highly theoretical, given that for much of their history, Jews had little choice but to follow the decrees of non-Jewish authorities. Their very lives and the life of their community depended upon such compliance. Nonetheless, classical teachings insist upon the importance of community authorization even for Gentile leaders.

According to Rabbi Samuel ben Meir (ca. 1080–1174), for example, the only reason Jews must follow a non-Jewish king is that his subjects have empowered him to rule, and, therefore, his decisions are binding.

> All taxes, rates, and rules of kings' law commonly established in their kingdom are law, for all subjects of a kingdom willingly accept the king's laws and statutes. Therefore they are perfectly valid law.[26]

In a similar fashion, Moses Maimonides argued that the leadership of a non-Jewish sovereign is legitimate only when his

> . . . coins circulate in the localities concerned, for then the inhabitants of the country have accepted him and definitely regard him as their master and themselves as his

servants. But if his coins do not circulate in the localities in question, he is regarded as a robber who uses force, and as a troop of armed bandits, whose laws are not binding.[27]

Whether or not the views expressed in these texts reflect a realistic understanding of the Jewish predicament in medieval Europe, there can be little doubt that they do suggest a distinctively Jewish approach to leadership. Even Gentile kings cannot simply assume control over others. Their powers, like those of every leader, must first be authorized in order to be considered legitimate.

Judaism's insistence that leadership must operate with the simultaneous sanction of both God and the people has left a legacy for all future generations of Jewish leaders. On the one hand, the only way to claim authenticity is to affirm a bond with the work of prior leadership types (already sanctioned by God), even when portfolios are radically different. Thus, when Maimonides sought to defend the legitimacy of the Babylonian exilarchs, for example, he advanced the persuasive argument that, "The exilarchs of Babylon stand in the place of the king. They exercise authority over Israel everywhere . . ."[28] On the other hand, as noted, it was equally important to affirm the support of the people, because the tradition understands that no leader can succeed without the buy-in of his or her followers.[29] As the rabbinic sages taught in the name of Rabbi Isaac, "A leader is not to be appointed unless the community is first consulted."[30]

In eighteenth- and nineteenth-century Europe an unusual leadership model, the hasidic *zaddik*, arose that combined these two precepts in a fascinating way. The *zaddik* (*rebbe* in Yiddish) was a true charismatic, believed by his followers to have the gift of divine grace. This blessing allowed him to serve as the conduit between his followers (*hasidim*) and God. He was their redeemer, protector, and intermediary. Only he was capable of achieving true *devekut* (adhesion to God). By aligning with their *rebbe*, the *hasidim* would be elevated to spiritual heights never available to them on their own. The *zaddik* had powers that were unique among humans. Through his prayers barren women would become fertile, business failures would be reversed, and the sick would be healed.

Given the strong bond presumed to exist between the *zaddik*'s powers and God, it would be surprising if his followers played even a minor role in empowering his leadership. Yet, it was precisely the support of his *hasidim* and their authorization of his powers that allowed the *zaddik* to lead. Absent *hasidim*, there could be no *zaddik*. Had his charismatic powers not been recognized, acknowledged, and continually sanctioned by his followers, the mere claim of divine blessing would have proven vacuous and grossly insufficient.

Far from being controversial or embarrassing, appreciation of the fact that the *rebbe* was dependent upon his *hasidim* was the source of great celebration and inspiration to the early hasidic masters. *Hasid* and *zaddik* were analogized to matter and form, or body and soul, suggesting that each was incapable of functioning without the other. The *zaddik* without his *hasidim* was a lonely man without a mate, not a commanding leader of his people. In his study of hasidic literature, Martin Buber observed: ". . . the zaddikim need the multitude, and the multitude need the zaddikim. The realities of hasidic teaching depend on this inter-relationship."[31]

The late-eighteenth- and early-nineteenth-century hasidic authority, Israel Friedmann (1797–1850), known as Israel of Ruzhin, likened the *zaddik* and *hasid* to the letters and vowels of the Hebrew alphabet. Without the authorization of his followers, the *rebbe*'s leadership would be worthless, much as an unvocalized Hebrew text remains inchoate and undecipherable. The famed hasidic rabbi, Yaakov Yosef of Polnoy (d. ca. 1782) offers an even more dramatic acknowledgment of the import which communal authorization has in legitimating a leader, even a charismatic one. "The *zaddikim* are . . . the first two letters of the Divine Name. The common people are the last two letters," he wrote.[32] This is an enormously powerful teaching about leaders and followers. The reference is to what is known as the tetragrammaton, the four letter Hebrew name of God—YHWH. Yaakov Yosef here suggests that communal authorization is not only necessary for effective leadership, but it has cosmic consequences, as well. Specifically, when the *zaddik* (YH) is empowered by his *hasidim* (WH), the oneness of God is reaffirmed and His holy name (YHWH) is unified.

The complexities of such a mystical interpretation notwithstanding, the overarching point should be clear. Even the *hasidim*, who were firmly convinced that their leader was the beneficiary of special blessings from God, recognized and lauded the fact that divine approval is not enough. Jewish leaders require the sanction of the community as well.

While Jewish sources are unambiguous in asserting that credible leaders are accountable both to God and their followers, this traditional understanding appears to have little resonance with those who hold titled positions in today's Jewish community. The very idea that their work as Jewish leaders is somehow linked to God and to premodern constructs of divinely sanctioned leadership would surely strike many as preposterous. While they are, of course, committed to the missions of the synagogues, federations, and organizations they serve, few Jewish leaders—lay or professional—see any linkage between their activities *as Jewish leaders* and a sense of accountability to the Divine.

One of the by-products of modernity is that leading in Jewish life has been deracinated from its theological framework. In sharp contrast to the traditional view that understands communal leadership and godliness to be part of a holistic interrelationship ("He who occupies himself with communal needs is as one who occupies himself with the study of the Torah"),[33] many in today's Jewish community see any attempt to frame leadership in these terms as cause for concern. Today's Jewish leaders are often ill-equipped and unprepared to explore the theological roots of their work. Moreover, they fear that excessive "God-talk" will alienate secular Jews or brand them as some form of fundamentalists.

On the other hand, the idea that leaders also owe their powers to the authorization of the community ("You must know whether they have in fact been approved by the people . . . a man should not be considered for office until people sing his praises),"[34] appears equally as alien a concept to many contemporary Jewish leaders. For some who work in the community's sacerdotal arena, for example, God's imprimatur seems all the authorization they need. Accountability to followers strikes them as an unnecessary constraint upon, and impediment to, their leadership. For others, whose work as Jewish leaders is tantamount to "returning a favor," or noblesse oblige, the idea of community sanction seems an annoyance, if not a gross intrusion. Many of these Jewish leaders would likely have agreed with Theodor Herzl (1860–1904), who observed, "I am still willing to do something FOR the Jews—but not WITH the Jews."[35]

In contemporary America, this gap between the theory and practice of Jewish leadership continues to grow and to wreck havoc upon the community. As mentioned previously, large numbers of today's Jews have chosen to walk away from the communal infrastructure altogether. Disaffected by the pettiness and bureaucracy of the "system," many are blissfully unaffiliated and completely disinterested in the very individuals or groups that claim to represent them. Disappointed in their rabbinic, educational, and philanthropic leaders, scores of thoughtful and caring Jews continue to seek spiritual meaning and personal relevance outside the institutions of the organized Jewish world.

For these searching Jews the cavernous disconnect between Jewish leaders and the classical teachings of Judaism is particularly disheartening. Many yearn, albeit unknowingly, for the very types of leaders called for by the tradition—leaders, not bureaucrats; moral and ethical exemplars, not technicians; responsive and impassioned listeners, not those who simply seek to superimpose out-of-date templates upon an already radically changed world. In short, today's Jewish community would benefit immeasurably from authentic Jewish leaders, accountable to both God and the community.

Those who occupy important positions in the Jewish world ought to consider the implications of these teachings for their own work. To the degree that lay and professional officials may have taken either God or the people for granted, they would be well advised to consider the ramifications of their attitudes, particularly in light of current demographic and attitudinal trends. Throughout Jewish history, even the most secular of leaders drew inspiration and vision from the belief that their leadership was authorized as part of a continuous chain that extended all the way back to the Torah itself. A leader's behavior and worldview were informed by the understanding that how they conducted themselves was of enormous consequence to both God and their coreligionists. Whether they were wealthy philanthropists or highly credentialed communal employees, they were unwilling to forsake their responsibility to either God or the people. Such an approach allowed them to innovate and respond to changed circumstances while remaining authentic Jewish leaders. Those who hold titled positions today should ask how their actions compare to this standard. Even as their leadership reflects current realities, is it consistent with the best of earlier models? Is their work informed by a sense of transcendence and spirituality? Are they cognizant of the needs of their followers and dedicated to working with the entire community? In large measure, the willingness to ask (and answer) these questions is critical for all those who aspire to be authentic Jewish leaders.

Despite the potential of human leaders to usurp God's role and hoard power, classical Jewish sources, inspired by the example of God Himself, are unwilling to categorically forbid such leadership. Indeed, when mandated by conditions of the time, postbiblical Jewish authorities allowed the development of radically new models of communal leadership with greatly expanded powers. While God's status as the only absolute leader remained secure and inviolable, Jewish sources reflect a realistic understanding of the need to extend leadership deep into areas never anticipated by the Torah.

Importantly, however, the methodologies by which these powers were expanded make it clear that those who lead, including those who lead in the twenty-first century, are bound to both God and the people. For those who might be inclined to proclaim self-righteously that God's sanction (or familial connections, or wealth or status) is justification enough for their leadership, Judaism reminds them that no leader can afford to ignore the needs of his or her followers and succeed over the long term. At the same time, Jewish leaders become effective leaders only when their work incorporates a sense of the Godly—an acknowledgment that power is not absolute, that leadership is fleeting, that no leader is above the law, that followers are not subordinates but human beings created in the image of the divine, and that ultimately, leadership is a gift from God. This ought to be as true in the contemporary period as it was in the ancient world.

The requirement that power must be authorized both by God and the people thus becomes a means of simultaneously legitimating and circumscribing leaders. Those who claim the mantle of authentic Jewish leadership today must strive constantly to fulfill their obligations to both the celestial and the terrestrial realms. Such a balanced perspective allows Jewish leaders to acknowledge the connection between God and their leadership without ignoring the needs of their followers or succumbing to religious fanaticism.

NOTES

1. For a description of leadership in the biblical period see my *Models and Meanings in the History of Jewish Leadership* (Lewiston, NY: The Edwin Mellen Press, 2004), 23–46.

2. Deuteronomy 18:2.

3. Jeremiah 1:4–6. Also see the opening chapters of Ezekiel, Amos, and Jonah.

4. See II Samuel 15:2–4.

5. II Samuel 7:11–16.

6. Leviticus 8:1–3.

7. II Samuel 5:1–3.

8. I Kings 12:1.

9. II Kings 11:17–20.

10. Abraham J. Heschel, *The Prophets* (New York: Perennial Classics, 2001), 23.

11. I Kings 18:17–40.

12. Rodney R. Hutton, *Charisma and Authority in Israelite Society* (Minneapolis: Fortress Press, 1994), 131.

13. Moses Maimonides, *Mishneh Torah*, Laws of Kings 3:8; 4:1; 4:10; 5:3.

14. Menachem Meiri, *Beit ha-Behirah, Sanhedrin* 20b.

15. *Avot* 1:1.

16. *Bava Batra* 12a.

17. For more on this, see Byron L. Sherwin, *Workers of Wonders* (Lanham, MD: Rowman & Littlefield Publishers, Inc., 2004), 31–43.

18. *Bava Metzia* 59b.

19. See *Bava Kamma* 84b, *Gittin* 88b, *Sanhedrin* 24a–b, *Mishnah Megillah* 3:1, Jerusalem Talmud, *Megillah* 74a. Also see Menachem Elon, *Jewish Law—History, Sources, Principles*, Volume I (Philadelphia: The Jewish Publication Society, 1994), 20–29.

20. *Gittin* 36b. Also see *Yevamot* 89b.

21. Solomon b. Abraham Adret, *Responsa* 3:411.

22. Elijah Mizrahi, *Responsa* 53.

23. For an analysis of the legislative functions accorded the medieval Jewish community, see Gerald J. Blidstein, "Individual and Community in the Middle Ages: *Halakhic* Theory," in *Kinship and Consent: The Jewish Political Tradition and Its Contemporary Uses*, ed. Daniel J. Elazar (New Brunswick, NJ: Transaction Publishers, 1997), 327–69.

24. Gershom ben Judah, *Responsa* 97.

25. See, for example, Salo Baron, *The Jewish Community*, Volume II (Philadelphia: The Jewish Publication Society of America, 1948), 3–51; Daniel M. Swetschinski, *Reluctant Cosmopolitans: The Portuguese Jews of Seventeenth-Century Amsterdam* (London: The Littman Library of Jewish Civilization, 2000), 190–91; and Eric Zimmer, *Harmony and Discord: An Analysis of the Decline of Jewish Self-Government in 15th Century Central Europe* (New York: Yeshiva University Press, 1970), 14–29.

26. Samuel ben Meir on *Bava Batra* 54b.

27. Moses Maimonides, *Mishneh Torah*, Laws of Robbery and Lost Property 5:18.

28. Moses Maimonides, *Mishneh Torah*, Laws of Sanhedrin 4:13.

29. The Italian biblical commentator, Obadiah ben Jacob Sforno (ca. 1470–ca. 1550), reflected this idea in his commentary on Exodus 28:41. Before Aaron and his sons could fully assume their positions as priests, Sforno argued, they had to be "completed" by their followers.

Highly respected leadership experts from the general academic community have adopted a similar sentiment in recent years. See, for example, the classic article by Robert E. Kelley entitled, "In Praise of Followers," Reprint, *Harvard Business Review* (November-December 1988), 1–8. Kelley's concept of "effective followers" bears a striking resemblance to Ronald Heifetz's idea of "leaders without authority." See Ronald Heifetz, *Leadership Without Easy Answers* (Cambridge, MA: Harvard University Press, 1994), 181–231.

30. *Berakhot* 55a.

31. Martin Buber, *Tales of the Hasidim—Early Masters* (New York: Schocken Books, 1947), 7.

32. Yaakov Yosef, *Zafnat Paneah* 48d. For more on Yaakov Yosef, see Samuel H. Dresner, *The Zaddik* (Northvale, NJ: Jason Aronson, Inc., 1994).

33. Jerusalem Talmud, *Berakhot* V, I, 8a.

34. *Sifre* Numbers 92.

35. From the *Diaries of Theodor Herzl*, cited in Ernst Pawel, *The Labyrinth of Exile* (New York: Farrar, Straus & Giroux, 1980), 239. Similar things were said of Louis Marshall; see my *Models and Meanings in the History of Jewish Leadership*, 276.

Chapter Three

Limiting Power

The requirement that leaders must be sanctioned both by God and the people is, in and of itself, no guarantee that power will be used wisely or appropriately. Jewish sources recognize that there is a widespread tendency to abuse the trappings of public office, even when a leader's powers are fully authorized and lawful. With complete candor, classical Jewish religious writings acknowledge that claiming the imprimatur of God and the people is no surety against pretense and sanctimony. In fact, the knowledge that God and the people have authorized one's powers might actually lead to an increased sense of imperiousness and triumphalism. In a system that encourages present-day leaders to see themselves in the same mold as their venerated predecessors, the risks of haughtiness and self-aggrandizement are significant.

To this end, the Torah insists that a leader's powers be severely circumscribed. In part, this is a logical extension of Judaism's assertion that only God is absolute. No human leader can be allowed so much power as to endanger or attenuate divine hegemony. Moreover, the potential to misuse power exists with all leaders, and those with the greatest powers are actually the most inclined to abuse them. As the Talmud teaches, "The greater the man, the greater his Evil Inclination."[1] Since in Judaism, every human being, whether follower or leader, is created *b'tzelem elohim*, in the image of God, the proclivity to lord power over others cannot be tolerated.[2] The best way to prevent followers from being mistreated, therefore, is to restrict their leaders.

One of the ways that the Torah sought to restrain human leaders is by insisting upon a strict separation between the three paradigms of biblical leadership (priest, prophet, and king). Not only was each typology assigned specific areas of responsibility, but important restrictions were established that proscribed one group from performing the duties of the others. In this way, power was simultaneously shared and circumscribed. By containing individual leadership types, the Torah guaranteed the inclusion of multiple

41

perspectives and militated against autocracy by refusing to allow total power to coalesce in a single group or individual.

The *kohanim* (priests), for example, while accorded considerable responsibility as the nation's sacral specialists, were expressly forbidden from ruling, that function being reserved exclusively for the monarchy. In explaining this restriction, the philosopher, Baruch Spinoza (1632–1677), notes:

> Now if, along with these [sacral] functions, he [Aaron, the priest] had held the right of issuing commands, his position would have been that of an absolute monarch. But this right was denied him . . .[3]

Interestingly, the one notable premodern exception to this separation between sacerdotal and political powers proved disastrous for the Jewish people. During the Hasmonean period (second to first centuries BCE), when priests were permitted to rule, the nation fell victim to widespread Hellenistic influences and teetered on the precipice of complete destruction.

The priests were not alone; biblical prophets were banned from holding any official post, as well. Indeed, one of the criteria by which the Bible established the veracity of a prophet is proximity to the ruling authorities. Simply put, a prophet suspected of being too close to the king could not be a real prophet of the Lord. For centuries after the close of prophecy, the spirit of these restrictions continued to inform their successors, the rabbis. In the majority of cases, the rabbinical sages of the talmudic period also held no community office. In fact, most were employed at other jobs—their work as sages being distinct from any recognized communal position. This situation continued well into the Middle Ages where many of the greatest scholars (*gedolim*) held no public title or station. As late as the twelfth century, the medieval legalist Moses Maimonides condemned community rabbis who viewed their work as an official métier, and sought compensation. Arguing that those who teach God's word in the tradition of the prophets should be above such considerations, he contended, "It is forbidden to derive any temporal advantage from the words of the Torah."[4]

The most highly restricted of all biblical leadership models was that of the king. Precisely because the Torah recognized that those with the greatest power were most likely to abuse it, it placed very specific limitations upon the monarch's duties and activities.

> Be sure to set as king over yourself one of your own people; you must not set a foreigner over you, one who is not your kinsman. Moreover, he shall not keep many horses or send people back to Egypt to add to his horses . . . And he shall not have many wives, lest his heart go astray; nor shall he amass silver and gold to excess. When he is seated on his royal throne, he shall have a copy of this Teaching written

for him on a scroll by the levitical priests. Let it remain with him and let him read in it all his life, so that he may learn to revere the Lord his God, to observe faithfully every word of this Teaching as well as these laws. Thus he will not act haughtily toward his fellows or deviate from the Instruction to the right or to the left to the end that he and his descendants may reign long in the midst of Israel.[5]

The book of II Chronicles adds to the restrictions placed on the sovereign. In summarizing the well-known story in which Azariah, the priest, confronts King Uzziah for exceeding his duties, the text notes the following:

The priest Azariah, with eighty other brave priests of the Lord, followed him in and, confronting King Uzziah, said to him, "It is not for you, Uzziah, to offer incense to the Lord, but for the Aaronite priests, who have been consecrated to offer incense. Get out of the Sanctuary, for you have trespassed; there will be no glory in it for you from the Lord God."[6]

As the priests were restricted from ruling and the prophets prohibited from holding public office, the king's responsibilities were also limited. A sovereign cloaked in a cultic mantle, who claimed to be above the law, was a despot in the making, and just as dangerous as a religious leader who sought the powers of governance.

Postbiblical authorities reinforced and even added to these early restrictions on the monarch. In sharp contrast to non-Jewish practice, Judaism insisted that, regardless of how legitimated his powers, the sovereign is always subordinate to God, the "king of all kings." As Maimonides said, "When there is a conflict between the edict of the Master (God) and the edict of the servant (the king), the former takes precedence over the latter."[7] In general, all talmudic and medieval limitations on monarchial powers can be understood as attempts to preserve the preeminence of God's rule, by further separating the political function from the religious one, or as efforts to militate against a single individual acquiring too much power. Thus, the Talmud specifically forbids the king from serving as a judge and from being given a seat on the national court, the Sanhedrin. He is further proscribed from participating in panels that were charged with setting the liturgical calendar.[8]

Maimonides explained that the reason kings are forbidden from serving as judges, and even witnesses in a court of law, is "because they are arrogant."[9] As a result, he imposed severe limitations on the king's conduct and interpersonal behavior, beyond those already specified in the Torah.

He must not exercise his authority in a supercilious manner . . . He should deal graciously and compassionately with the small and the great, conduct their affairs in their best interests, be wary of the honor of even the lowliest. When he addresses the public collectively, he shall use gentle language . . . At all times, his conduct should be marked by a spirit of great humility . . . He should put up with the cumbrances, burdens, grumblings, and anger of the people . . .[10]

The Spanish talmudist Nissim Gerondi (ca. 1310–1375) also addressed this particular monarchial limitation.[11] Just as priests were prohibited from legislating and prophets were proscribed from holding office, the king, he argued, was forbidden from serving as a judge. To Gerondi, this restriction makes sense because of the divergent standards that applied to judges and kings. "This is the difference between magistrate and king: the magistrate is more bound to the Torah's laws than is the king." For this reason, he argued, the king was specifically commanded to keep a copy of the Torah by his side (Deuteronomy 17:18–19). Gerondi continues, "Since the king sees that he is not bound to Torah law as the judge is, he must be strongly admonished not to deviate from its commandment . . . The magistrate, however, requires no such admonition, since his power is restricted by the scope of Torah law alone . . ."

Maimonides and Gerondi thus provide valuable insight into how Judaism approaches the question of a king's abuse of power. Recognizing that the risk of such excess is endemic to monarchy, precisely because the greater the power, the greater the chance for its abuse, they each reflect Judaism's pragmatism on this issue. Rather than bemoan the human tendency to hoard power, or eradicate kingship completely, the Torah, they argue, anticipates these problems and then seeks to attenuate their impact by imposing clearly articulated restrictions on the powers of all kings. In Gerondi's words, "Since his power is mighty and induces arrogance, God admonishes [the king] not to 'act haughtily toward his fellows' (Deuteronomy 17:20)."

Though most of the writings that sought to restrict the duly authorized powers of the king were concerned with Jewish sovereigns, some applied a similar standard to Gentile kings, as well. While, arguably, these particular texts were more theoretical than practical, they do provide important insights into the tradition's insistence that a leader's power must be contained. According to these sources, Gentile rulers had influence over Jewish subjects only in areas not covered by Jewish religious law. As far back as the Talmud, the principle was articulated that Jews were obligated to follow the law of the land, provided that it did not conflict with identifiably religious precepts.[12] As the author of the legal compilation, *Sefer ha-Terumot*, observed the rabbinic principle that 'the law of the land is the law' (*dina de-malkhuta dina*) applies:

. . . only to those matters that are the king's interests, such as roads, customs duties, and other taxes, but as to private matters between individuals the Sages did not say that the "the law of the land is law." . . . As to the affairs of a Jew with his fellow Jew, we are not to judge between them by the law of the kingdom . . .[13]

Just as the powers of the Jewish king were circumscribed by religious law, so too, those of the Gentile king. From the perspective of traditional Jewish sources, the local sovereign's powers were broad and encompassing, but not absolute. What was true for all other leaders was true for him as well; even pervasive powers have their limits.

While attempting to contain the Gentile sovereign by restricting his sphere of influence to nonhalakhic matters may seem the most that could possibly be achieved under the circumstances, Jewish sources went further in their attempts to mitigate the abuse of non-Jewish monarchial authority. Here the sources manifest what may be considered either a boldness of spirit or an incredible naiveté. Summarizing general rabbinic opinion on this issue, Moses Maimonides outlined Judaism's approach. The king, he acknowledged, is permitted enormous powers, with considerable latitude. So long as his decrees do not call for the violation of a religious tenet, his law is the law. Ostensibly, he can do whatever he wants. And then comes a rather notable exception.

> The general rule is: any law promulgated by the king to apply to everyone and not to one person alone is not deemed robbery. But whatever he takes from one particular person only, not in accordance with a law known to everyone but by doing violence to this person, is deemed robbery.[14]

Simply stated, the king, even with all of his powers, is not permitted to behave arbitrarily. He is proscribed from the indiscriminate administration of justice. He is not allowed to have one set of standards for certain subjects and a different set for others. What is true for the subjects is true for the king—all are bound by the law. The stereotype of a capricious monarch indiscriminately bandying about his powers, bestowing favors in one corner and behaving rashly in another, is anathema to Jewish understandings of effective leadership. No Jewish source doubts or even minimizes the potency of the monarch, but his powers are not without limits. Even the greatest leader in the land is not permitted to abuse power.

That these teachings had little practicable impact is largely beside the point. Centuries of living with the scourges of indiscriminate rule combined with a sacred tradition that mandated limited powers for all leaders gives Jewish insights into power and leadership particular poignancy. While non-Jewish kings may not have been bound by these high standards, Jewish communal officials certainly were. If the Gentile sovereign was obligated to curtail his power and guard against its abuse, how much more so were the leaders of the local Jewish community similarly obliged?

These sources on monarchy make it clear that a profound awareness of the dangers of unrestrained power permeates Judaism's approach to leadership.

No one is above the law, arrogance has no place in the relationship between leaders and followers, and too much power in any one set of hands is a prescription for disaster. The Bible and later authorities went to great lengths to contain the excesses of high office. The particular restrictions articulated are not random but rather reflect a clear understanding of a leader's natural tendency to want more control and greater influence. They provide safeguards in the very areas in which power is most likely to be misused.

Just how insightful and apposite these ancient restrictions are becomes clear when they are evaluated in light of the previously cited research of Dr. Arnold Ludwig. As noted, in his discussion of the "Perks of Power," the term he used to describe "benefits" that accrue to those who rule, Ludwig found that political leaders worldwide have an increased likelihood of access to sex, wealth, and deference as a result of their positions. Not surprisingly, these "perquisites" are particularly prone to high levels of abuse by those in power. Significantly, these are precisely the areas that the Torah and subsequent Jewish sources sought to limit when restricting the powers of the monarchy. Reconsidered in view of Ludwig's findings, then, Judaism's classical restrictions on the king reveal uncanny astuteness. Because, either by guile or coercion, the ruler could have any woman he wanted (recall David and Bathsheba),[15] the Torah says, "And he shall not have many wives." Because the sovereign needed funds for an array of purposes—some in the public interest and some not—and because he could acquire those funds any way he wanted, including by impoverishing his subjects (consider the case of King Ahab and the vineyard of Naboth),[16] the Torah instructs, "Nor shall he amass silver and gold to excess." And, precisely because the adulation and obsequiousness that were permanent features of the king's reign would lead to hauteur and condescension, the Torah insists that he keep a copy of the law with him at all times so as not to "act haughtily toward his fellows."

Before examining how postbiblical Jewish authorities interpreted and applied the Torah's attempts to circumscribe power in their own communities, it should be admitted that such restrictions come with a price. The approach to human leadership woven throughout the Bible, and adapted by later Jewish sources, created a leadership tradition that, at best, is far less efficient than conventional top-down, command-and-control models. (As many will recognize, this is an oft-cited charge frequently leveled by entrepreneurs and corporate leaders when first asked to join a board or committee in their local Jewish community.) In its preoccupation with unbridled power and the consequent insistence that priests, prophets, and kings be proscribed from performing each other's duties, the Torah encouraged a system in which contentiousness and division are inevitable. By demanding that religious leaders not rule and political leaders not officiate, Judaism set the stage for an approach to governance that is often bureaucratic, ineffective, and tedious. The requirement that leadership functions be separated frequently results in enterprises that are plodding and deliberative and individuals whose leadership work is often characterized by high levels of competition and jealousy. (Many contemporary Jewish leaders would acknowledge that such a tradition persists to this very day.) Resulting entities are rarely well suited to rapid and unified communal mobilizations, particularly in times of extreme crises. Centralized responses are difficult in a system that is committed to decentralization as a matter of principle.

Nonetheless, as will be seen in the section that follows, later Jewish authorities remained convinced that the admixture of religion and politics is too volatile. Avoiding autocratic rule and maintaining the unequivocal supremacy of God far outweighed the putative benefits associated with models alleged to be more efficient.

The Bible's concern that a leader's powers be limited inspired subsequent generations of Jewish thinkers to remain vigilant against the excesses of human authority. Talmudic sages, for example, imposed clearly defined boundaries upon their own work, despite having gone to great lengths to legitimate their roles as community leaders. As noted in the previous chapter, without apology, they arrogated for themselves the right to interpret Jewish law. But, at the same time, they limited their powers by disallowing anything considered to be innovation.

> It is clearly and explicitly set forth in the Torah that its ordinances will endure forever without variation, diminution or addition . . . Accordingly, if any one should arise, whether among the Gentiles or among the Israelites, and showing a sign and token, declare that God had sent him to add a precept to the Torah or take away a precept from the Torah, or give an interpretation to any of the commandments, such as we had not heard from Moses; or should assert that the commandments ordained to Israel are not of perpetual obligation for all generations but only temporary, such a man is a false prophet . . . He is to be put to death . . .[17]

Rhetorical as this restriction surely was (the work of the talmudic rabbis being both legislative and juridical), the traditional understanding is that prohibitions against changing the law were important and valuable constraints upon the otherwise exhaustive powers of the sages. In a further attempt to prevent their own excesses, the rabbis of the Talmud forbade any activity that would place unnecessary hardship on the people. "We make no decree upon the community unless the majority are able to abide by it."[18] Maimonides explained the ramifications of this precept:

> Before instituting a decree or enacting an ordinance or introducing a custom which it deems necessary the court should calmly deliberate and make sure that the majority of the community can live up to it. At no time is a decree to be imposed upon the public which the majority thereof cannot endure . . .
>
> If the court has issued a decree in the belief that the majority of the community could endure it, and after the enactment thereof the people made light of it and it was not accepted by the majority, the decree is void and the court is denied the right to coerce people to abide by it.[19]

These Jewish leaders clearly understood that their own success was not advanced by categorical pronouncements or dictatorial acts. Having already established their right to lead (by linking themselves to Moses and the prophets, as described in chapter 2), they had no further need to flex their juridical muscles and impose unnecessary strictures. Rather, they recognized the natural tendency for those who lead to misuse power and then took significant steps to prevent themselves from doing so.

Similar sensibilities informed Jewish life throughout the Middle Ages, where wealthy community trustees (*parnasim*), local rabbis, and erudite scholars often engaged in hostile internecine battles in an attempt to constrain what each group considered to be the others' abuses of power. Rarely were these arguments about the illegitimate acquisition of leadership, per se. Rather, those involved in such heated debates understood what the Torah had earlier made clear, namely that even when power is fully legitimated it is prone to abuse. The task of all responsible leaders, therefore, is to guard against such extremes both within themselves and among those with whom they share responsibility for governance.

It should be noted that while Jewish writings from the Middle Ages are filled with vituperative exchanges between Jewish leaders on the subject of power excesses, not all of these are such noble attempts to guard against abuses. In point of fact, many reveal as much about those doing the accusing as those being accused. While charges about hoarding power and misusing position or wealth, for example, abound in the literature of the period, it becomes clear that such lofty arguments are often power plays of their own. When lay people sought to constrict the responsibilities of community rabbis, and rabbis sought to legislate against lay involvement in communal policy-making, the issue often had less to do with circumscribing power and more to do with advancing the interests of a particular leadership group. Nevertheless, the language and message of these disputes resonated with a people that had long been sensitized to guard against leaders who abused the powers of their office.

An analysis of these restrictions reveals many of the same themes, regardless of which group is being chastised and which is leveling the attack. Communal leadership is understood as a sacred charge. Precisely because these posts were believed to be sanctioned by God and the people, occupants were duty bound to control their rampant inclinations to power. Merely having the legal right to do something, for example, assess taxes (lay councils), issue legal rulings (rabbinical courts), and so forth does not excuse mistreating others or the inappropriate use of one's position. Several examples will prove illustrative.

For most of the Middle Ages, it had been established that councils of wealthy lay people were empowered to govern the internal affairs of the local Jewish community (see chapter 2). "The community can take action in order to meet the needs of the moment."[20] Nevertheless, because even legitimated powers can be abused, many rabbis sought to contain this right of the laity. One of the most well-known examples comes from Rabbi Solomon ben Abraham Adret (Rashba) who challenged a lay council's ability to tax a resident who owned property in two different communities. Adret argued that while the laity had legitimacy to tax, it had no right to abuse its authority by taxing the same person twice.

> The argument that the community can enact laws in such matters seems to me to be no more than robbery, and unjust enactments are not valid . . . It is not within the power of the community unjustly to deprive anyone of his money and appropriate it for communal use.[21]

Adret's message is clear: among those who wield power, the tendency to exceed the limits of appropriate behavior is omnipresent.[22] Consequently, continued awareness of and attendant vigilance to the natural inclinations of human leadership are in order.

Rabbis before and after Adret also found it necessary to restrict the powers of the local lay leadership who, while accorded certain rights, were perceived as consistently overstepping their bounds. The famed commentator Solomon ben Isaac (Rashi, 1040–1105) is a notable example. In his day, in medieval France, wealthy *parnasim* were empowered to invoke a ban (*herem*) upon errant members of the community. The power to place an individual in *herem* was extremely significant since, in a world in which religion governed every aspect of one's existence, excommunication meant social ostracism, economic ruin, and even sometimes death. In Rashi's view, such powers were too great, and too easily prone to abuse when vested in the hands of lay people. Despite its widespread practice and prior authorization, he denied *parnasim* the right to issue such bans, insisting that doing so was the exclusive province of rabbinical authorities instead.[23]

Moses Maimonides put forth a similar argument in his attempt to restrict lay jurists. While acknowledging that lay people had a perfect right to serve as judges and to make certain decisions regarding communal governance, he insisted that these powers applied only when there was no great sage residing in the community. If a sage was present, these otherwise legitimate powers of the laity were automatically invalidated.[24]

At the core of each of these restrictions was a growing concern on the part of the rabbis that affluent lay people were usurping their authority and displacing learning and piety as communal priorities. Because wealth is such a potent and influential force in leadership, many rabbinic authorities strove to limit its impact by severely constraining the rule of the laity in all facets of communal governance. In 1681, for example, Rabbi Jacob Sasportas (1610–1698) issued the following statement describing the insidious tendencies of the lay leaders of Livorno, Italy.

> They [the Livorno leaders] . . . seized power for themselves through their wealth and might, finding favor by transferring silver . . . Money reigns supreme, the deficient [man] gains an appointment and is deemed a[ppropriate].[25]

Nearly a century later, rabbis were still concerned that wealthy lay leaders were misusing their powers, permitting the corrosive effects of money to destroy the soul of Jewish life. According to Rabbi Yaakov Yosef of Polnoy:

> This is, alas, the situation between the leaders of each generation and the wealthy of every city . . . In every generation, the rabbis and other learned men want to strengthen our faith, teaching the people the path upon which they should walk and the deeds which they should perform, by the light of the Torah . . . But there are those coarse persons, swollen in pride, who despise the learned who seek to walk before them . . . Thus it is written in the Talmud: "Jerusalem was destroyed only because the people despised the learned . . ."[26]

To many rabbis of the period, the single most egregious abuse of lay power was to be found in the way the *parnasim* treated them. The sixteenth-century mystic Rabbi Judah Loew of Prague (1525–1609) criticized lay leaders for intimidating local rabbis by refusing to award employment contracts longer than three years at a time. *Parnasim*, he charged, kept rabbis under tight reins, forcing them to live in perennial fear of losing their jobs.[27] Loew's successor as Chief Rabbi of Prague was Ephraim Luntshitz (1550–1619), who also accused lay leaders of exceeding the limits of their authority.

> Besides, in their pride they actually deem themselves free from all faults and sins, in very truth paragons of virtue. And so, they are bent on muzzling their [rabbinical] leaders. The power of election is in their hands. They can always find men of more

tractable disposition. They purposely elect their rabbi for a short term so that, dominated by the motive of fear, he may tamely submit to their wishes. And should the courageous leader dare to expose the follies and offences of the people, ignoring their intimidations and successfully defying their evident power, he will soon discover that even though firmly entrenched in his position he has been worsted in the struggle nonetheless. For his opponents, numerous and unprincipled, will be sure to invent and rehearse scandalous stories most damaging to his character, stories which once widely circulated must sooner or later neutralize the whole effect of his preaching.[28]

In truth, the claims of these rabbis were not without merit. *Parnasim* were often far more interested in controlling the rabbinate than in partnering with them. The inclination to abuse their powers and their wealth is, as charged, documented in the rabbinical employment contracts that have been preserved from the period. While some European communities proffered terms that were quite generous and supportive, many others went to extreme lengths to limit the powers of their rabbis. They had to promise not to interfere in secular affairs, not to seek extensions of their contracts, and to support the *parnasim* in all of their rulings, even if they ran counter to the will of the community.[29] The following excerpts from sixteenth-century Italian rabbinical contracts shed light on some of these attempts.[30]

> . . . [W]e, the two lay leaders of the city . . . accept and take upon ourselves as leader, prince, judge and teacher the distinguished rabbi, Rabbi Johanan son of Saadyah . . . the distinguished rabbi shall be required every day, early in the morning, following the conclusion of the prayer in the synagogue, to teach the Talmudic text to those who wish to hear it; he shall also be required to do so every day, for one hour or more, prior to the Afternoon Prayer . . . And he will not be allowed to teach more than seven hours a day at most, and the rest of the time . . . he shall peruse and involve himself with matters which are to the benefit of the holy community, to chastise, to set aright, and to punish those who behave wrongly . . . And he shall be required, upon the request of the Holy Congregation of Verona or of the majority of the leaders at the time, to enact or to ban or to agree to whatever matter or edict [they may ask] . . .

While it is not unusual for employment agreements to stipulate particular duties, many of these contracts specifically limited the amount of time the rabbi could devote to teaching his students while simultaneously mandating him to execute whatever the lay leadership desired. Another example comes from the community of Casale.

> It was decided . . . that for the next two years, the Distinguished Rabbi . . . should be the rabbi of the Holy Community . . . with the condition that he may not decide concerning financial questions regarding members of the community without the agreement of the two lay leaders . . .

As any contemporary congregational rabbi can attest, attempts by lay leaders to "clip the wings" of the rabbinate are hardly unique to the medieval epoch. A famous modern example comes from the illustrious career of the well-known American rabbi, Stephen Wise (1874–1949). Rabbi Wise was appointed to the prestigious pulpit of Temple Emanu-El in New York City. In 1905, he was informed by the lay leadership of that congregation that "it was considered as a necessary condition, applicable to any incumbent of the office of rabbi in the congregation, that the pulpit should always be subject to and under the control of the Board of Trustees." To the resounding cheers of his colleagues, even a century later, Rabbi Wise refused to tolerate such bonds. He left the congregation, though not before responding that "The chief office of the minister as I take it is not to represent the views of the congregation, but to proclaim the truth as he sees it . . . ."[31]

As the foregoing examples make clear, attempts on the part of both lay leaders and rabbis to restrict each other's powers have a long and complicated history. As far back as the biblical period and continuing to present day America, religious and political leaders have strained to respect each other's legitimacy while protecting against their excesses. In some cases, such restrictions are rooted in a deep concern that unbridled power simply cannot be tolerated; it is bad for the community and an abrogation of God's command. In others, the motivations that led rabbis to constrain lay leaders and laymen to bind rabbis can only be described as self-serving. In all cases, however, there is an underlying value system mirrored in such efforts. Jewish writings on leadership reflect a realistic understanding that strong leaders—lay and rabbinic—easily habituated to the allure and approbation of their office, often see themselves, or are seen by others, as demigods. They are frequently driven by a natural desire to increase power and control. Without the sensibility occasioned by these restrictions, most leaders remain blinded to the manifold ways in which power is abused.

It is not that Judaism opposes strong leaders or that the purpose of the previously reviewed constraints is to cripple those in office. Judaism, however, begins with an assumption that because human beings are not God, their leadership will, by definition, be flawed. These leaders, predisposed to want more and more power, are hard pressed to impose limitations upon themselves. The inclination to lord power over others, even to the point of misuse, is not limited to a small fraction of nefarious leaders. All who hold power walk a thin line; all are susceptible to self-aggrandizement and arrogance. All must guard with vigilance against the excesses of their work, not because they are evil, but because leadership is vulnerable and it brings with it an increased risk of abuse.

Judaism understands that power, even if it is held legally, with all the requisite authorizations is still susceptible to misuse. Indeed, the irony is that sanction by God and the people often becomes a source of false pride, leading to increased haughtiness and sanctimony. No leadership type is exempt or immune from such concerns. The possibility of autocracy and condescension exists whether the individual in question is a spiritual leader or a political one. To this end, the hasidic literature points out that even the greatest religious leaders have within them the potential for abuse of power.

> The word "Rabbi" (*Ra-bi*) can be interpreted through its initials. If one who becomes a rabbi is sincere and dutiful he is *R*osh *B*'nei *I*srael, a leader of the Children of Israel or "*r*evered of the *b*egotten of *I*srael." If he is insincere and neglectful of his duties, then he becomes *R*a *B*'ayney Adona*I*, *R*epellent (to those) *B*eloved by the *I*mmortal One.[32]

In the aggregate then, these insights led to the creation of an extensive series of constraints upon leaders. Designed to prevent too much power from being held by any single individual or leadership type, such restrictions militate against the rise of despotic or tyrannical rule within communities and organizations. To be sure, such limitations have not always been driven by noble intentions; often they represented attempts to suppress the powers of one group in order to elevate those of another. Nor is such an approach always the most effective, if efficacy is measured by harmony, consensus or unity of purpose. In general, however, those were never Judaism's major concerns for leaders. Far more important were the goals of serving the needs of followers, empowering leadership in others, and creating a society and a world in which only God's rule was absolute.

Contemporary Jewish leaders have much to learn from the wisdom of the tradition. The truth is that very few of the men and women who hold leadership positions in today's Jewish world spend any time at all contemplating the implications of this material. At a minimum, it seems appropriate that those who lead the community begin to consider the possible misuses of their own power. Jewish teachings make clear that, ipso facto, leadership increases the likelihood of hoarding and abusing power. This is true whether one is an elected official or a congregational rabbi. It certainly applies in a broader context, as well. Physicians and soldiers, executives and professors, all those in power need to be sensitized to these issues. Leaders must be taught about the risks of abusing power in order to avoid doing so. Judaism leaves no doubt that those who wield the greatest authority—over worshipers, students, patients, investors, employees, or citizens—are precisely those who are most susceptible to excesses, even unknowingly.

For these reasons, leaders are duty bound to approach their work with vigilance and care. Leadership training—whether seminary education, workshops for lay people, or executive development—must heighten a leader's awareness of the potential for such abuse and help provide the necessary antidotes for combating these inclinations. Individuals who do not reflect upon these issues as part of their own leadership work—either as professionals or volunteers—fail to don the authentic mantle of Jewish leadership. Jewish organizations and communities must incorporate systemic protection against the aggrandizement and misuse of power by any and all who occupy titled positions within the enterprise.

NOTES

1. *Sukkah* 52a.
2. Genesis 1:26.
3. Baruch Spinoza, *Tractatus Theologico-Politicus*, trans. Samuel Shirley (Leiden: E. J. Brill, 1991), 257.
4. Moses Maimonides, *Mishneh Torah*, *Talmud Torah*, 3:10. Similar sentiment is expressed in *Avot* 4:7.
5. Deuteronomy 17:15–20.
6. II Chronicles 26:17–18.
7. Moses Maimonides, *Mishneh Torah*, Laws of Kings, 3:9.
8. *Sanhedrin* 18a–b.
9. Moses Maimonides, *Mishneh Torah*, Laws of Kings, 3:7.
10. Moses Maimonides, *Mishneh Torah*, Laws of Kings, 2:6.
11. Nissim Gerondi, *Derashot* 11. Translated and cited in Michael Walzer, Menachem Lorberbaum, and Noam J. Zohar, eds., *The Jewish Political Tradition*, Volume I (New Haven: Yale University Press, 2000), 156–61.
12. *Bava Kama*, 113a–b.
13. *Sefer ha-Terumot*, Gate 46, Chapter 8.
14. Moses Maimonides, *Mishneh Torah*, Laws of Robbery and Lost Property, 5:14.
15. II Samuel 11.
16. I Kings 21.
17. Moses Maimonides, *Mishneh Torah*, Foundations of the Torah, 9:1.
18. *Avodah Zarah* 36a.
19. Moses Maimonides, *Mishneh Torah*, Rebels, 2:5–6.
20. Rabbi Solomon Abraham Adret, *Responsa* 2, 279.
21. Adret, *Responsa* 5, 178.
22. A similar message appears in the writings of Adret's student, the fourteenth-century Spanish rabbi, Joshua ibn Shu'eib. In his sermons, Shu'eib insisted that community leaders must consistently protect against the excesses of pride, arrogance, pursuit of honor

and power, even when their authority was legitimately established. See Carmi Horowitz, *The Jewish Sermon in 14th Century Spain: The Derashot of R. Joshua ibn Shu'eib* (Cambridge, MA: Harvard University Press, 1989), 37–54.

23. Solomon Zeitlin, "Rashi and the Rabbinate," *Jewish Quarterly Review* Volume 31 (1940–41): 36–7.

24. Moses Maimonides, *Mishneh Torah*, Laws of Sales 14:9–11. Maimonides based his decision on a similar ruling in the name of the talmudic sage Rav Papa; see *Bava Batra* 9a.

25. Jacob Sasporatas, "Letter and a Critical Circular," cited in Walzer et al., *Jewish Political Tradition*, 429.

26. Yaakov Yosef, *Toldot Yaakov Yosef*, Lemberg Edition, 103c, cited in Samuel H. Dresner, *The Zaddik* (Northvale, NJ: Jason Aronson, Inc., 1994), 77.

27. Byron L. Sherwin, *Mystical Theology and Social Dissent* (London: Associated University Presses, 1982), 167–69. Rabbi Loew was also extremely critical of his rabbinical colleagues whose sycophantic behavior, in the interest of protecting their own pecuniary interests, served to enable such exploitation.

28. Israel Bettan, *Studies in Jewish Preaching* (Cincinnati: Hebrew Union College Press, 1939), 286. Like his predecessor, Luntshitz excoriated the rabbinate for "excessive timidity" and accused them of "protecting their own honor" rather than God's. (Bettan, 287.)

29. Salo Baron, *The Jewish Community*, Volume 2 (Philadelphia: The Jewish Publication Society of America, 1948), 86–87.

30. Cited in Robert Bonfil, *Rabbis and Jewish Communities in Renaissance Italy* (London: The Littman Library of Jewish Civilization, 1993), 331–35.

31. Cited in Simon Schwarzfuchs, *A Concise History of the Rabbinate* (Oxford: Blackwell, 1993), 146–47.

32. *Sippurei Besht* (Warsaw: A. J. Kleiman, 1911), 15.

Chapter Four

Power-Sharing

Driven by the knowledge that leaders with too much power undermine divine rule and destroy the very organizations they allege to serve, Judaism, as seen, sought to contain such excesses by limiting the powers of those who lead. The tradition's unique approach to leadership, however, is not just about disabling power hungry autocrats. Rather, it is informed by the firm belief that separating leadership functions and requiring power to be shared is a far more effective and beneficial way to lead than having a single, all-controlling individual sit alone at the head of an enterprise.

The virtues of sharing power are presented throughout Judaism's classical texts without the slightest hint that such an approach contributes in any way to the diminution of a leader's influence, efficacy, or reputation. To be sure, the sources recognized that power-sharing is a compromise in which the outcomes are far from guaranteed. Nevertheless, its benefits far outweigh the potential uncertainties.

God Himself sets the tone for all leaders when He willingly gives up some of His power to enable the leadership of human beings, in spite of the inherent risks. In this context, readers will recall the previously examined biblical text (I Samuel 8) in which God agrees to authorize monarchy. Notwithstanding His considerable reservations, God chooses to reduce His own potency for a greater good: the need for leadership in human society. In so doing, He transmits a critical lesson. Shared power is not antithetical to strong leadership; it is its essence. Just as a burning flame can be used to kindle many candles, without ever diminishing its own light, so strong leadership is not diminished by sharing power with others.

A similar message is conveyed in a text first analyzed in chapter 2. In the Talmud's discussion of the oven of Akhnai (*Bava Metzia* 59b), God is portrayed as happily retreating from His role as author of the law. When the sages insisted that, once the Torah was given, legal answers are no longer to

be found "in heaven," God stepped back in order to allow the rabbis suffi-
cient room to lead. Far from diminishing His influence, by sharing power,
God was actually guaranteeing the continuity and dissemination of His work.
God's example thus becomes a model for all who wish to lead.

The mystical tradition of sixteenth-century Safed provides yet another perspective on power-sharing in leadership. According to the renowned kabbal-
ist, Isaac Luria (1534–1572), in the process of creating the world, God
deliberately contracted Himself in order to make room for human beings to
be His partners in this important work. The eminent theologian, Rabbi
Eugene Borowitz, has suggested that in this idea of divine contraction (*tzimtzum*), God offers a model for all human leaders. Those who lead, he argues,
would do well to emulate God by deliberately curtailing their own powers in
order to develop and nurture the leadership potential in others. To be sure,
doing so has certain risks, including the possibility that followers may not
remain true to the original plan; they may go off and lead in a different direction. That having been said, however, the benefits of raising a new generation
of leaders, trained to think independently, willing to venture out on their own,
are redemptive; the functional equivalent of what the mystics called *tikkun*
(repair). This can only be accomplished by embracing the power-sharing
principle in leadership. Curiously, but incontrovertibly, when leaders share
powers with others, they are not diminished; they are, in fact, enhanced.

> So the parents who see their children able to make their own decisions maturely,
> though they choose a peculiar lifestyle; so the teachers who see their students
> become competent scholars, though they reach conclusions at variance from what
> they were taught; so the clergy who develop laymen committed to living religiously,
> come what may, though they transform the traditions they received; such leaders by
> *tzimtzum* know they have done as much as men can do to save a troublesome and
> treacherous world.[1]

Unquestionably, sharing power is difficult for leaders. Few people are
comfortable being second-guessed. Many feel that having arrived at a certain
stage in their lives or careers they shouldn't have to compromise on their
decisions. Oftentimes, leaders have worked hard to get where they are, and
the idea of sharing power with those believed to be less skilled or less experienced is demeaning. Power-sharing may sound like the right thing to do, but
in reality, when tough choices have to be made, no one wants to risk bad
decisions by empowering others.

Resistance of this sort is hardly unique to the contemporary world. Classical Jewish sources make it clear that even Moses, thought to be the most
enlightened and thoughtful of all leaders, struggled with many of these same
issues. The tendency for leaders to want to do things themselves, rather than

depend on the skills and judgments of others, is as natural as it is dangerous. Leaders often feel that they must do it all—fix all the problems and answer all the questions. Not only is such an approach a prescription for disaster, as no single individual can do everything, it is a sure way to foster dependence among followers, not build leadership in others. Aggrandizing power, even if driven by a sincere desire to "do things right," may accomplish a short-term goal, but from a Jewish perspective, is not effective leadership.

For Moses, this inclination to share power did not come naturally; it had to be taught to him by his father-in-law, Jethro. Yet, once learned, it proved to be among the most important lessons of his life and career.

> But when Moses' father-in-law saw how much he had to do for the people, he said, "What is this thing that you are doing to the people? Why do you act alone, while all the people stand about you from morning until evening?" Moses replied to his father-in-law, "It is because the people come to me to inquire of God. When they have a dispute, it comes before me, and I decide between one person and another, and I make known the laws and teachings of God." But Moses' father-in-law said to him, "The thing you are doing is not right; you will surely wear yourself out, and these people as well. For the task is too heavy for you; you cannot do it alone. Now listen to me. I will give you counsel, and God be with you! You represent the people before God: you bring disputes before God, and enjoin upon them the laws and the teachings, and make known to them the way they are to go and the practices they are to follow. You shall also seek out from among all the people capable men who fear God, trustworthy men who spurn ill-gotten gain. Set these over them as chiefs of thousands, hundreds, fifties, and tens, and let them judge the people at all times. Have them bring every major dispute to you, but let them decide every minor dispute themselves. Make it easier for yourself by letting them share the burden with you. If you do this—and God so commands you—you will be able to bear up; and all these people too will go home unwearied."[2]

Interestingly, when asked to explain his willful concentration of power, Moses defends himself by blaming the people, "It is because the people come to me . . ." Like many leaders, he has convinced himself that no one is capable of doing what needs to be done except for him. While he derives considerable advantage from his position as the man with all the answers, his "need to be needed" impedes his efficacy. Exhausted and ineffective as he surely must have been, he simply could not conceive of an alternate approach. In truth, however, as Jethro points out, power hoarding is neither good for Moses nor for the very people he wants to lead. Leaders may think they are doing the right thing for their followers by coalescing all decision-making, but in truth, "The thing . . . is not right."

To Moses's credit, however, he learned this essential lesson in leadership well. In the words of the text, "Moses heeded his father-in-law and did just as he had said."[3] As truly effective leaders will proudly attest, power-sharing begins with a willingness to take counsel from someone wiser, regardless of status or position. Leaders need partners—as advisers, mentors, and confidantes. Giving up the illusion that the leader can do it all, that she or he must have all the answers, is an essential step in this process.

The rabbis of the Talmud, who saw themselves as heirs to the Mosaic tradition, and who were unabashed in arrogating an array of their own leadership powers, were mindful, nonetheless, of the long-term benefits of power-sharing. Reverential as they were in their assessment of Moses, they recognized in his desire to centralize power a dangerous tendency. To underscore this point, the rabbis, in an audacious text, fabricated a dialogue between Moses and God in which Moses boldly expresses the desire for expanded personal powers. God, however, quickly disabuses Moses of his illusions, making it perfectly clear that power-sharing, not power-hoarding, is the best way to serve Him and the people. "Moses wished to have priests and kings descending from him, but God said . . . 'Your sons will not offer up sacrifices, for the priesthood has already been allotted to your brother Aaron . . .' and 'Kingship is already assigned to David . . .'"[4]

Here, the rabbis give expression to the view that a system of governance in which powers are separated, yet shared, is far more effective than a system in which a single great leader performs all leadership functions simultaneously. Precisely because strong leaders are not naturally predisposed to sharing power, Judaism designed a leadership system that forces them to do so. This critique of Moses is all that more remarkable because of the esteem in which he was held, and in light of the sages' own struggles with power, as they sought to establish their legitimacy as leaders of the Jewish people.

Other Jewish sources provide further evidence of the tradition's bias in favor of power-sharing. The ceremony by which a king of Israel was anointed provides a telling example. In describing the installation of King Solomon, the Bible records:

> So Zadok the *priest*, and Nathan the *prophet* . . . went down and caused Solomon to ride upon king David's mule and brought him to Gihon. And Zadok the priest took the horn of oil out of the Tent, and anointed Solomon. And they blew the ram's horn; and all the people said: "Long live *king* Solomon" (emphases added).[5]

In this text, the three biblical leadership models are all present—priest, prophet, and king. Each has a separate and distinct role to play in the leadership of the people; as discussed in the previous chapter, one leadership type cannot perform the duty of the others. At the same time, however, the text makes clear that effective rule of the polity can only happen when all three leadership models come together sharing power for the benefit of the people-at-large.

In the *Mishnah* another example of power-sharing is discussed. According to the rabbis, while separate powers are essential to the efficient operation of the nation, certain major functions can only take place when all leadership typologies work in concert. It is not that such power-sharing ventures require individual leaders to compromise or abandon their own unique perspectives and approaches. Rather, there is an overarching recognition that when diversified interests come together, the benefits to the nation as a whole are materially increased.

> No additions may be made to the City or the Temple Courts except by the decision of a *king, prophet, Urim and Tummim* [oracles found in the breastplate of the biblical high *priest*] and a Sanhedrin of seventy-one, and two thank-offerings and song (emphases added).[6]

While one might think that a decision to undertake a "building campaign" would be the exclusive purview of the king and his advisers, this *mishnah* makes clear that such a venture, like the anointment of the sovereign, has far-reaching ramifications and must, therefore, receive the thoughtful support of varied leadership perspectives. (Those involved in contemporary capital projects in the Jewish community will recognize the wisdom of such a teaching.) The decision to expand or build a facility is not merely an administrative matter. Beyond funding, there are a host of legal, religious, moral, and ethical issues to be factored into any such decision. While sharing power is often far more cumbersome than unilateral decision-making, its long-term advantages are significant.

Judaism's incontrovertible preference for power-sharing was not merely a theoretical position to be pondered and never acted upon. In point of fact, the enormity of sources extolling the merits of separate yet shared power meant that individual Jewish communities would be structured in ways that actualized the power-sharing ideal. As a result, beginning in the biblical period and continuing to the present day, Jews pioneered a system of communal organization in which: (1) leadership functions are separated; (2) no single leader ever amasses overarching control; and (3) divergent leadership interests are forced to share power for the ultimate good of the community.

The prototype for this model is found in the Bible itself. As seen, priest, prophet, and king had distinct roles, each endorsed by God and charged with specific areas of responsibility. No leadership type had complete authority. Kings could rule but not officiate at the sacrificial altar, priests controlled the cult but could not actually govern, and though they transmitted the word of God, prophets were proscribed from holding high office. When taken together, these three leadership typologies were responsible for the life of ancient Israel. Priest, prophet, and king brought the people closer to God, interpreted divine law for each new generation, and governed the civil affairs of the polity.

The biblical system of tripartite leadership laid the groundwork for what is known as the *ketarim* or "crowns" of leadership. Rooted in the rabbinic teaching that "There are three crowns (*ketarim*)—the crown of torah (*keter torah*), the crown of priesthood (*keter kehunah*) and the crown of kingship (*keter malkhut*),"[7] this idea became the pervasive paradigm for Jewish communal organization. Over the centuries of Jewish diaspora, beginning in Babylonia, continuing throughout Europe and North Africa, and in America as well, this three-pronged system of separate but shared leadership characterized most Jewish communities.

In each postbiblical generation, wherever Jews settled, the leadership of their communal enterprises was divided between those in charge of learning and education, those who oversaw religious practices, and those who governed the local civic affairs. To be sure, the individual crowns of leadership were continuously refashioned in every age, in response to radically altered circumstances. Thus, for example, the destruction of the two Temples (586 BCE and 70 CE) caused upheavals in the *keter* of *kehunah*, just as the emancipation of Jews in eighteenth- and nineteenth-century Europe occasioned major shifts in the status of those who wore the crown of torah. Additionally, the lines separating the *ketarim* were often blurred; some political leaders were also scholars, and sometimes rabbis had responsibilities for economic matters as well. Yet, with consistency this threefold system of communal leadership, in which power is at the same time separated *and* shared, has typified Jewish communities throughout history.

As might be expected in a tradition that seeks authenticity by linking present developments to past precedents, representatives of each *keter* sought to connect their work to earlier models, even when their portfolios had metamorphosed considerably. Thus, for example, contemporary congregational rabbis insist that they are bound inextricably to rabbis of premodernity. This, despite the fact that as "pastors," and (what has derisively been referred to as) "*brokha* brokers," they have precious little in common with their predecessors of the same title.[8] Similarly, postbiblical representatives of *keter malkhut*, known by a variety of titles, including *resh galuta* (exilarch) in Babylonia, *nagid* in Spain, *parnas* and *shtadlan* in medieval Europe, and philanthropist and communal professional in modern America insisted that they too were part of an ongoing tradition that traced all the way back to the biblical kings. (In fact, such an argument is not so far-fetched if one considers that these leaders, including today's fund-raisers, volunteers, and communal executives—like the ancient monarchs—had responsibilities for revenue collection, defense, external relationships, and governance.)

According to the groundbreaking research of the late Daniel Elazar, generally considered to be the dean of Jewish political studies, in this "ketaric" system, each crown claims its own source of authority and asserts its right to function independently.[9] Not surprisingly, therefore, tensions, competition, and what might be called inter-ketaric rivalries are omnipresent. Despite such animus, however, the entire system is interdependent. While each *keter* passionately asserts its claim to communal hegemony, the goal is not the eradication of the other *ketarim*. The biblical prophets (*keter torah*) sought to temper an out-of-control monarchy (*keter malkhut*), not to eliminate kingship altogether. When, in the Middle Ages, wealthy *parnasim* (*keter malkhut*) sought to circumscribe the role of the local rabbi (*keter torah*), they were not challenging the rabbinate's fundamental right to adjudicate, only what it perceived to be its desire to dictate communal policies and procedures. When contemporary congregational rabbis (*keter kehunah*) decry local federation leaders (*keter malkhut*), they do not deny the inherent worth of the system, only its claims of absolute centrality.

While ketaric equilibrium may never have been achieved to perfection, the lessons of Jewish history suggest that, in order for a Jewish community to function properly, all three *ketarim* must be present. To be sure, the balance of power has oscillated over the millennia between priestly preeminence, rabbinic dominance, and an all-controlling laity. Yet underlying the entire system is an acknowledgment that a community is not well served unless and until all leadership interests are represented at the table of communal discourse.

Given the pervasiveness of the power-sharing precept in classical Jewish texts, it should come as no surprise, then, that over time, leaders of the various *ketarim* found ample opportunities to work together, despite the profound differences in their worldviews. One of the most dramatic examples of power-sharing comes from the medieval period and pertains to the issuance of the *herem*, the ban of anathematization, placed upon errant members of the Jewish community.[10] Not surprisingly, both rabbis and *parnasim* claimed the right to issue such bans, independent of one another. Rabbis insisted that, as a religious document, decisions about issuing or rescinding a *herem* were theirs alone. *Parnasim* felt strongly that since the imposition of a ban had economic ramifications, the rabbis had to impose or withdraw such an edict whenever instructed to do so by the governing lay council. While strong theoretical arguments in support of each position were mounted, the realities of the day interceded and militated the adoption of a shared approach when such dramatic action was required. Because of the *herem*'s severity, concerns were raised both about its capricious use and the potential for retaliation by a banned party. Rabbis, therefore, sought the imprimatur of the laity before taking such extreme steps, and lay councils acknowledged the importance of having such bans authorized by well-respected rabbis. While neither rabbis nor *parnasim* abandoned their unique perspectives on how to lead the community, in reality, both came to recognize that at critical times, power-sharing, even when it meant compromising on matters of turf, was a far more effective way to lead. As a result, throughout most of Europe unilateral declarations of the ban were attenuated, and power-sharing became an operating principle.

> It was now decided that the Rabbi should have no power to declare any excommunication without the consent of the community, nor should the community have the power to excommunicate any member without the consent of the Rabbi.[11]

The supracommunal organizations of medieval Europe represent another significant example of power-sharing. Also referred to as supercommunal organizations, synods, and committees, or *va'adim*, in Hebrew, these umbrella groups of communal councils (*kehillot*) from Poland, Lithuania, Moravia, and Hungary functioned from the last half of the sixteenth to the early eighteenth centuries. The most famous of these was the Council of The Four Lands (*Va'ad Arba Arazot*), which represented Jewish communities in Great Poland, Little Poland, Podolia, and Volhynia. These supracommunal organizations were designed, in part, to unify geographically proximate *kehillot* on a diversity of religious and political matters. Included in their discussions were issues of tax collection, combating anti-Semitism, and assisting distressed Jewish communities, along with a broad gamut of halakhic matters, ranging from oversight of ritual slaughterers to regulations on book publishing. The leadership of these organizations was shared between rabbis and lay people, representing the constituent *kehillot*. Official decisions and pronouncements of these bodies were issued jointly in the name of both rabbis and *parnasim* to alleviate any confusion or conflict and to disseminate a unified message. The historian Jacob Katz analyzed the *takanot* (enactments) emanating from these organizations and concluded that:

> Indeed, there was no clear-cut demarcation between the lay and rabbinical spheres of authority: the *parnasim* assisted in ensuring the dominance of religion in public life, and they were assisted in turn by the rabbis, the preeminent representatives of religion, in enforcing the *takanot* in other spheres . . . In their public proclamations, the lay and rabbinic leaders appeared as virtually a single entity. The rabbis did not hesitate to sign regulations pertaining to economic or political matters; indeed, it

was assumed that they approved of the lay leaders' decisions unless they actively objected. It is not mere happenstance that even though the *parnasim* did not necessarily solicit the active assistance of the rabbis, they couched their proclamations in religious terminology . . .[12]

Thus, without compromising the underlying principles that guided their work, rabbis and lay leaders agreed to share power for the betterment of the communities they served. *Parnasim* not only knew Torah and revered learning, they respected the halakhic authority of their rabbis. At the same time, rabbinical leaders acknowledged and deferred to the potency of the laity when it came to advancing and improving the economic and political lives of the people. They didn't always agree, but they understood that by sharing power they were, in fact, strengthening their own leadership and the communities they represented.

In modernity, a version of power-sharing informs the organizational structure of the American synagogue movements as well. While three of the four major congregational groupings trace their roots to nineteenth-century Europe, all four (including Reconstructionism) reached their zeniths in twentieth-century America. Despite the enormous differences in theology, ideology, practice, and style, each movement is structured in a remarkably similar fashion. In each, there is an organizational infrastructure that roughly corresponds to the ketaric rubric. Orthodox, Conservative, Reform, and Reconstructionist rabbis all have an official movement seminary.[13] These institutions, embodying the contemporary crown of torah, educate their students in subjects deemed appropriate for today's Jewish clergy. Secondly, in addition to a seminary, each movement has an organization (or multiple organizations) designed to serve the professional needs of the rabbis, cantors, and other representatives of *keter kehunah* in matters that range from continuing education to career placement and retirement planning.[14] Finally, those lay and professional leaders who wear the contemporary crown of kingship, as synagogue board members, committee chairs, administrators, and officers, are served by a third arm of each movement: the umbrella organization of affiliated congregations.[15]

No one familiar with the inner workings of any of today's synagogue movements would suggest that these three arms work together in complete concord. Hostilities between the three *ketarim* remain palpable even in the twenty-first century; to this degree the movements have more in common than might be supposed. The point is not that all three leadership typologies see the world the same way. On the contrary, they do not, they never have, and they should not. At the same time, however, no synagogue movement can succeed without power being shared between the respective ketaric representatives.

In the broadest sense then, what are often derided as stereotypical internecine battles—tensions between academics and philanthropists, congregational rabbis and federation board members—are, in fact, evidence of a
thriving and healthy system of communal leadership. While mocking the
contentious relations among and between the *ketarim* is often the stuff of
which great Jewish humor is made, such jokes point to something that is actually quite profound.[16] Amidst all the derision and ridicule, there is a clear
sense that leadership in Jewish life is not a monolith and that what is often
bemoaned as dysfunctional Jewish behavior is, in fact, evidence that functioning Jewish communities avoid autocracy by mandating power-sharing.
The fact is that when Jewish leaders—spiritual, educational, or political—do
their jobs on behalf of the Jewish people, they are likely to "lock crowns"
with equally passionate representatives of the other *ketarim*.

The prevalence of classical sources advancing the idea of power-sharing in
leadership should not, by any means, suggest universal Jewish compliance
with these teachings. On many occasions, Jewish communities experienced
and supported the rise of single leaders who sought, either overtly or subtly,
to don all three crowns at one time. These individuals, who expressly rejected
the power-sharing precept, are referred to by a variety of descriptors—
messianic, mystical, or charismatic leaders. Throughout history, they bore a
diversity of titles; in some communities they were known as *hakham* (among
the German pietists of the twelfth and thirteenth centuries), *mashiah* (by followers who believed that their arrival signaled the final redemption), *zaddik*
(by eighteenth- and nineteenth-century *hasidim*), or *da'at torah* (by ultra-
Orthodox Jews in modernity).[17]

In each case, leaders of this type share several important characteristics.
The charismatic (almost always a man) is believed by his followers to be
endowed by God with supernatural or superhuman powers.[18] (The English
word charisma comes from the Greek meaning "gift of grace.") These powers enable the leader to "fix" or resolve a crisis that the regnant leadership
system has been impotent to address. The link between catastrophe (or perceived catastrophe) and the salvific abilities of the leader is essential in a
charismatic relationship. The promise of a better future, and the knowledge
that only the leader can bring this about, helps to explain his successes.
Importantly, the individual in question normally holds no official position in
the community; nor is he compensated from communal funds. Indeed, more
often than not, he defines himself *in opposition* to the establishment. In Jewish communities, this almost always involved an excoriating critique of the
dominant rabbinic and lay leadership.

Such individuals had no interest in power-sharing; they brooked no dis-agreement from followers or critics. Indeed, theirs was a cult of personality. Followers were encouraged to pledge and manifest absolute fealty. Because of the leaders' unique gifts, there could be no such thing as separated powers. By definition, no one else had the abilities and genius they possessed. They were peerless, and for this reason, their opinions and pronouncements were binding, even on matters that appeared to far exceed their areas of particular responsibility.

With consistency, important Jewish communities have embraced charis-matic leaders over the centuries. Their influence cannot easily be dismissed, despite sharp contrasts with the ketaric model. In point of fact, messianic movements in Judaism, from Jesus of Nazareth to Shabbetai Tzvi (1626–1676), have consistently attracted large numbers of adherents who, when faced with unspeakable crises and despair, were relieved to know that a single leader had emerged with a promise of rescue and renewal. In return, followers were prepared to radically alter their lives at the leader's behest. Similarly, Jewish mystical and *hasidic* leaders, from Judah the Pietist (1150–1217) to Habad's Menachem Mendel Schneerson (1902–1994), united their followers and inspired them to tackle seemingly insurmountable tasks with a passion and dedication that would make any leader envious. In the modern period, certain exceptional Orthodox rabbis, including Moshe Feinstein (1895–1986), Aaron Kotler (1892–1962), and Joseph Soloveitchik (1903–1993), were believed by their acolytes to be blessed with *ruah hakodesh*, the holy spirit. As such, their *ex cathedra* declarations, on issues that went far beyond *halakhah*, were embraced and transmitted with a palpable fervor.

As proof of the durability and potency of this model, today even some non-Orthodox thinkers have discussed the benefits of its restoration, particularly with regard to American synagogue life. They argue that the rabbinate's loss of status and prestige in America is attributable to the fact that the rabbi is no longer looked upon as a charismatic "holy person."

> The contemporary American emphasis on making religious institutions more demo-cratic, egalitarian, accessible, informal, and politically correct has weakened the social stature and religious authority of the clergyperson.[19]

In this view, only when rabbis are charismatic, in the classical sense of the word, will the rabbinate return to its position of reverence, esteem, and effi-cacy. "If American clergy want to reclaim the power, prestige, and social status they once enjoyed, they must reclaim the wonder-working features of their job description."[20]

In modern Jewish history, charismatic leadership has not been limited to the purely religious realm alone. The most well-known example of a secular single leader who succeeded in attracting unprecedented numbers of enthusiastic followers was Theodor Herzl. Revered by his devotees, Herzl was characterized as a latter-day Moses and the "new Messiah," who would lead his people back to the Promised Land. He was notorious for his unwillingness to share power or to even consider ideas if they were not his own. His diaries reflect that he thought of himself as priest, prophet, and king, all rolled into one. He stood in sharp contrast to the mainstream rabbinic and philanthropic leaders of his day, whom he derided as cowardly and ineffectual. Persistent to the point of obsession, he engendered the loyalty of thousands of European Jews and succeeded in advancing the Zionist dream against all apparent odds.[21]

That Judaism can claim a number of such leaders in every epoch cannot be denied. That such an approach to leadership has its own successes is also a matter of historical record. In truth, the single leader model has produced a variety of significant accomplishments. Few other leadership styles generate the level of emotional investment on the part of followers or the consistently high performance goals realized in service to a leader. Further, nothing is as effective in mobilizing unified responses in times of crises and in focusing widely disparate forces on a single plan of action. In view of the linkage between charisma and crisis and the long history of crises that Jewish communities have had to endure, it would be imprudent to dismiss such leadership categorically. Moreover, the lessons learned during the Holocaust when the Jewish world was too fractured and paralyzed to mount a unified response, when no single leader arose to take charge, serve as permanent reminders that power-sharing has inherent weaknesses.

Yet, despite the appreciable upsides of the single leader model, Jewish teachings remain overwhelmingly predisposed to power-sharing as a more effective approach to leadership in the long term. In addition to the previously described theological and ethical objections to leaders with too much power, the "lone wolf" approach is extremely risky from the perspective of sustained efficacy. Simply put, single leader models, in general, and charismatics, in particular, fail to build effective leadership among followers.[22] The lessons of Jewish history are that in the overwhelming number of cases, the visions and dreams of charismatic leaders are evanescent; they and the entire enterprise often collapse with the death or retirement (or apostasy) of the leader. Because single leaders are often more concerned with personal "monument building" than with developing leadership in others, it becomes harder to transmit and sustain their work in the next generation. When followers believe that an individual is unilaterally capable of "fixing" their problems, they are disinclined to take responsibility for their own fates. Such an approach often leads to myopic and risky decision-making. Followers, who would be advisers, are reticent to share counsel, and leaders are less interested in hearing alternate perspectives. Blind tenacity and single-minded drive to actualize the leader's vision often result in disaster.

While the ketaric system of separate, yet shared power, is hardly without its own limitations, it alone provides communities and organizations their best protection against the rise of dictatorial single leaders. The evidence is overwhelming that when any one *keter* is permitted complete and total dominance, or when any one individual tries to wear all three crowns simultaneously, the overall enterprise suffers. This is as true in contemporary America as it was in ancient Israel or medieval Europe.

Despite the esteemed tradition of power-sharing and ketaric balance, in modern Jewish communities the "crown of kingship" has often been allowed to supplant both of the other leadership paradigms. Over the last two hundred years, as a result of a number of factors commonly identified with modernity (e.g., the need to replace a compulsory tax base with voluntary philanthropy, the decline of rabbinic authority and the attendant diminution of widespread Jewish learning, and the acceptance of Jews as full citizens in their countries of residence) the leadership of most Jewish communities has shifted disproportionately to *keter malkhut*, to those who excel at running campaigns—fund-raising, building, membership, and lobbying. Such an imbalance is both inauthentic and discontinuous. Not surprisingly, significant numbers of Jews who do care about the crowns of "torah" and "priesthood" are becoming increasingly disenfranchised with this approach to communal leadership. Unless today's Jewish communities seek to restore ketaric equilibrium in which learning, spirituality, *and* philanthropy each play a significant role, more and more of today's so-called Jewish leaders will find themselves becoming "generals without armies."

American Jewish communities must learn the lessons of Jewish history. Power-sharing is not tokenism; it cannot be effectuated merely by a panel on synagogue-federation relations or by inviting a professor of Jewish Studies to speak at a conference. Power-sharing begins with a recognition that each *keter* has a legitimated right to lead and is authorized to be at the table, not as an invited guest, but as an equally sanctioned representative of God and the Jewish people. If communities are to be led as *Jewish* communities, and not merely as communities of Jews, then no single *keter*, however invaluable, can be allowed to dominate the communal agenda.

Ketaric disequilibrium in modernity is not solely the by-product of an out-of-control *keter malkhut*. The contemporary synagogue also provides a telling example of what can happen when the principle of power-sharing is abandoned. Unlike their predecessors of earlier epochs, modern rabbis are often called upon to don all three crowns of leadership simultaneously. First and foremost, today's rabbi is engaged in the duties of *keter kehunah*—hospital visits, counseling, officiating at life-cycle ceremonies, and the conduct of worship services. She or he also works in the realm of *keter malkhut*—ambassador to the local government, advocate for Israel, official representative of the Jews in a variety of ecumenical contexts, along with frequently being the chief executive officer of the synagogue—raising funds, supervising staff, and advising lay committees. If any time remains, contemporary rabbis return to the world of *keter torah* to teach (although rarely to pursue their own scholarly interests). When one individual wears all three crowns, both leaders and followers pay the price. In the context of the evolution of the modern rabbinic portfolio, such developments may be understandable, but an all-controlling rabbinate is just as dangerous and unhealthy as a power-hoarding laity.

Ironically, one of the unintended, yet predictable, consequences of a rabbinate in which all three ketaric functions are centralized is a laity that is increasingly disempowered. Synagogue members, even trustees and officers, are often passive bystanders in the life of the synagogue, deferring to the view that the rabbi is in charge, and concluding that leadership in the congregational realm is already spoken for. Low levels of Jewish literacy in modernity leave many lay leaders feeling that their voice must be muted, if not silenced completely, because the rabbi knows more and spends more time at the synagogue than anyone else. Even in areas beyond what might be thought of as the rabbi's jurisdiction, congregational lay leaders are often encouraged to feel that their lack of Jewish knowledge obliges them to cede power and control. In this view, the rabbi is the surrogate for all things Jewish and is, therefore, exempt from sharing power.

For their part, many congregational rabbis find it difficult to collaborate with those who lack qualifications and learning and whose personal and professional schedules prevent them from devoting large amounts of time to the congregation. By training and socialization, rabbis often see themselves as the top of the pyramid, not as an equal component of the leadership triumvirate. The rabbis of old seemed to understand the complex interrelationship between financial/administrative leadership and scholarly/religious leadership when they taught, "Without sustenance, there is no Torah; without Torah there is no sustenance."[23] Modern rabbis, however, elevated high atop the congregational pedestal find that it is neither easy nor always desirable to come down and share power. For many, the very idea is insulting; doing so would irrevocably compromise their status.

Ironically, congregational rabbis often bemoan the disjuncture separating lay leaders from the religious, spiritual, and educational realms of the synagogue without ever realizing how their attempts to coalesce power may contribute to this sense of alienation. They criticize the fact that so many volunteer leaders remain fixated on matters of budget and administration without acknowledging how their own reticence to share power in the religious arena may exacerbate the laity's unwillingness to venture into areas where they feel unwelcome. Conversely, lay leaders often articulate that they want a "powerful" rabbi, yet they resent it when he or she amasses too much power. In the end, however, few of them are willing to assert their own status as representatives of an authenticated leadership paradigm, preferring instead to abdicate responsibility to the rabbi, albeit begrudgingly.

As is true for the larger Jewish community, synagogues, too, have much to gain by incorporating the power-sharing principle into their leadership structure. Today, some of the most exciting developments in what has come to be known as the "synagogue transformation" movement are proving beyond any doubt the virtues of power-sharing. In some rare cases, rabbis and lay leaders are moving beyond possessiveness and turf issues. They recognize that the success of the enterprise depends not on one *keter* outmaneuvering the other but on a willingness to share responsibility for leading the future of the congregation and its members. Rabbis and trustees must see themselves as leaders, not as competitors in a zero-sum game. When rabbis and board members understand that power-sharing does not imply weakness or abandonment of principles, a sense of ketaric balance can be restored.

In his important book on the subject, Rabbi Sidney Schwarz describes how several of today's American synagogues—across all movements and geographic boundaries—are being transformed by groups of Jewish leaders, lay and professional, rabbis and nonrabbis, who, in partnership with each other are leading their congregations to previously unanticipated levels of greatness.[24] In worship, outreach, social action, programming, and education, a handful of American synagogues—from the right to the left—are reinventing themselves because scholars, lay people, and rabbis are leading by sharing power. Rabbis, like the highly regarded Lawrence Kushner of Sudbury, Massachusetts, are redefining their jobs. Rather than seeking new opportunities to aggrandize power, these rabbis are willingly reducing their "powers" and concentrating their efforts on teaching members "how to run their congregation without rabbinic help. The rabbi," argues Kushner, "has to resist the temptation of regarding the congregation as a personal possession or fiefdom."[25] In return, lay leaders are not only learning more from their rabbi than ever before, but they are now invested in the congregation's worship services, educational programs, and ritual observances with a zest that exceeds the work they do on fiscal and managerial matters.

Power-sharing, whether in a local Jewish community or a synagogue, requires each *keter* to view itself as *a* leader, not *the* leader, of the enterprise. It begins by recognizing that power-hoarding is antithetical to effective leadership. Wearing all three crowns at once, or so disabling other *ketarim* that their inclusion is merely symbolic, serves neither followers nor God, nor empowers leadership in others.

NOTES

1. Eugene Borowitz, "*Tzimtzum*: A Mystic Model for Contemporary Leadership," in *What We Know About Jewish Education: A Handbook of Today's Research for Tomorrow's Jewish Education*, ed. Stuart L. Kelman (Los Angeles: Torah Aura Productions, 1992), 340.

2. Exodus 18:14–23.

3. Exodus 18:24.

4. Exodus Rabbah 2:7. Also see Deuteronomy Rabbah 2:7.

5. I Kings 1:38–39.

6. *Mishnah Shavuot* 2:2.

7. *Avot* 4:13.

8. Gerald Bubis, "Brokha Brokers and Power Brokers," *Jewish Spectator* 40, no. 1 (Spring 1975): 9–12. Similar sentiments have been expressed by many observers of the American rabbinate, including many well-known rabbis. Rabbi Irving "Yitz" Greenberg, for example, once decried the "administrator-fund raiser-benediction giver-pattern" plaguing the contemporary congregational rabbinate. See my *Models and Meanings in the History of Jewish Leadership*, 242, n. 699.

9. See Daniel J. Elazar and Stuart A. Cohen, *The Jewish Polity: Jewish Political Organization from Biblical Times to the Present* (Bloomington: Indiana University Press, 1985), 3–41. Also see Stuart A. Cohen, "The Concept of the Three *Ketarim*: Their Place in Jewish Political Thought and Implications for Studying Jewish Constitutional History," in *Kinship and Consent: The Jewish Political Tradition and Its Contemporary Uses*, ed. Daniel J. Elazar (New Brunswick, NJ: Transaction Publishers, 1997), 47–76.

10. Robert Bonfil, *Rabbis and Jewish Communities in Renaissance Italy* (London: The Littman Library of Jewish Civilization, 1993), 65–75; 111–17.

11. Louis Finkelstein, *Jewish Self-Government in the Middle Ages* (New York: Phillip Feldheim, Inc., 1964), 63–64; 242–43.

12. Jacob Katz, *Tradition and Crisis—Jewish Society at the End of the Middle Ages*, trans. Bernard Cooperman (New York: Schocken Books, 1993), 106.

13. The "movement seminaries" are not the only places where one can be ordained a rabbi either in the United States or internationally. Nevertheless, when the American synagogue movements refer to "their" rabbinical school they are almost always talking about

Yeshiva University (Modern Orthodox), Jewish Theological Seminary of America (Conservative), Hebrew Union College (Reform), or Reconstructionist Rabbbinical College (Reconstructionist).

14. Examples include the Reconstructionist Rabbinical Association, the Central Conference of American Rabbis (Reform), the Cantors Assembly (Conservative), and the Rabbinical Council of America (Orthodox).

15. These include the Union of Reform Judaism, the Union of Orthodox Congregations, the United Synagogue of Conservative Judaism, and the Jewish Reconstructionist Federation. In addition, in some of the movements, separate "trade" organizations serve the needs of professional congregational administrators as well.

16. Joseph Telushkin, *Jewish Humor: What the Best Jewish Jokes Say About the Jews* (New York: William Morrow and Company, Inc., 1992), 149–60.

17. There is an extensive literature on each of these leadership models. Readers wishing additional information on the German pietist *hakham* should consult Ivan G. Marcus, "Judah the Pietist and Eleazar of Worms: From Charismatic to Conventional Leadership," in *Jewish Mystical Leaders and Leadership in the 13th Century*, eds. Moshe Idel and Mortimer Ostow (Northvale, NJ: Jason Aronson Inc., 1998), 97–126; and Ivan G. Marcus, *Piety and Society: The Jewish Pietists of Medieval Germany* (Leiden: E. J. Brill, 1981). On messianism, see Marc Saperstein, ed., *Essential Papers on Messianic Movements and Personalities in Jewish History* (New York: New York University Press, 1992); and Stephen Sharot, *Messianism, Mysticism, and Magic* (Chapel Hill: University of North Carolina Press, 1982). Additional resources on the hasidic *zaddik* include Arthur Green, "Typologies of Leadership and the Hasidic Zaddiq," in *Jewish Spirituality from the Sixteenth-century Revival to the Present*, ed. Arthur Green (New York: Crossroad, 1989), 127–56; and Byron L. Sherwin, *Workers of Wonders* (Lanham, MD: Rowman & Littlefield Publishers, Inc., 2004), 93–119. For more on *da'at torah*, see my *Models and Meanings in the History of Jewish Leadership*, 255–63 and sources cited.

18. For more information on charismatic leadership, see Alan Bryman, *Charisma and Leadership in Organizations* (London: Sage Publications, 1992); and Max Weber, *The Theory of Social and Economic Organization*, trans. A. M. Henderson and Talcott Parsons (New York: The Free Press, 1947), 324–86.

19. Sherwin, *Workers of Wonders*, 2; 10.

20. Sherwin, *Workers of Wonders*, 125.

21. Ernst Pawel, *The Labyrinth of Exile—A Life of Theodor Herzl* (New York: Farrar, Straus & Giroux, 1980).

22. Readers should distinguish between "charisma" in its original sense (as defined earlier) and the conventional use of the term as a synonym for "magnetic" or "engaging."

23. *Avot* 3:21.

24. Sidney Schwarz, *Finding a Spiritual Home—How a New Generation of Jews Can Transform the American Synagogue* (New York: John Wiley & Sons, Inc., 2000). Also see *The Rabbi-Congregation Relationship: A Vision for the 21st Century* (Philadelphia: Reconstructionist Commission on the Role of the Rabbi, 2001), 15–22.

25. Schwarz, *Finding a Spiritual Home*, 65.

Chapter Five

Beyond the Great Man

Since becoming a recognized academic discipline, the study of leadership has inspired a number of important conceptual models. One of the earliest and most influential of these is known as the "Great Man Theory." In this view, leaders are distinguishable from followers based upon personal abilities and traits. Early studies sought to identify these attributes of leadership, asserting that they were inherent and could not be taught. They included such things as physiognomy (especially height) and sonorousness. Other factors believed to contribute to good leadership were wealth, birth order, and IQ.[1] According to the Great Man Theory, also referred to as the "lone wolf" approach or "heroic leadership," only certain individuals are predisposed to leading while others are not.[2]

As the name implies, the Great Man Theory exaggerates the importance of the individual leader. Other factors are minimized or discounted completely. Events are interpreted and refracted through the lens of the one in charge. The leader is depicted as the primary cause for why things happen or do not happen in an organization. In such a model, the success and failure of an entire enterprise rest largely upon the shoulders of the leader. To quote Thomas Carlyle, "The history of what man has accomplished in this world, is at bottom the History of the Great Men who have worked here."[3]

Perhaps the classic statement of heroic leadership is found in Napoleon's observation on war:

> Men are nothing; one man is everything . . . It was not the Roman army that conquered Gaul, but Caesar; it was not the Carthaginian army that made Rome tremble in her gates, but Hannibal; it was not the Macedonian army that reached the Indus, but Alexander.[4]

The Great Man Theory of leadership is decidedly hierarchical. In its most basic formulation, an individual at the top of an enterprise "influences" others on the lower rungs to *follow*. Sometimes the influence is overt and coercive; other times it is much more subtle. Sometimes the "followers" are referred to as "employees," other times by a variety of functionally equivalent terms: "members," "citizens," or "congregants." Implicit in this kind of leader-follower relationship is that the one at the top has something to *offer*, and that those who follow *depend* upon their leader for answers to their needs. On occasion, what is "offered" is concrete and measurable—a paycheck, physical protection, expertise. At other times, the offerings are more "magical," but no less significant—cures, validation, an inspired sense of purpose.

This top-down conception of leadership is thought to work best when certain distinct personality traits, commonly thought of as characteristics of good leaders, are also manifest. These include strength, magnetism, single-mindedness, and forcefulness. Heroic leaders are superhuman figures, dominating both competitors and followers. Their decision-making is unilateral—even arbitrary and indiscriminate. Having arrived at the top, these lone wolfs eschew accountability of any sort.

As Judaism has for centuries, today's most progressive leadership theories distance themselves from this archaic view. While the leader-as-talisman prototype may offer followers temporary comfort (and the leader a sense of inflated self-importance), long-term effective leadership is not about miracle working or command-and-control. Among contemporary leadership experts, the Great Man Theory is obsolete. Most would agree with Warren Bennis and Robert Thomas that we have reached the end of

> . . . the myth of the Lone Ranger—the belief that great things are accomplished by a larger-than-life individual shouting commands, giving direction, inspiring the troops, decreeing the compelling vision, leading the way, and changing paradigms with brio and shimmer.[5]

In place of the Great Man Theory comes a "newer" understanding of leadership, one that bears an uncanny resemblance to that which has always been at the core of Jewish teachings. This new research consistently corroborates Judaism's classical perspective, and suggests that adaptability, shared responsibility, and empowerment of followers, not *ex cathedra* pronouncements, lie at the core of effective leadership.[6] Those who nurture others, who "give the work back" to the people themselves, are far more likely to succeed than those who bark commands and unilaterally impose their will upon the organization.[7]

> [R]eal heroes are the leaders who work with followers as intimate allies. Intimacy and trust . . . cannot be achieved when leaders distance themselves from followers

or when leaders allow themselves to be distanced . . . At a moment in time when it seems like anyone can become a celebrity, heroic leaders may very well be the men and women who shun the spotlight and put followers first . . . The old command-and-control leadership is passé . . . Instead of commanding, today's leaders align, create, and empower.[8]

While it has taken modern leadership experts generations to come to the conclusion that "organizations are . . . something more collegial than the lengthened shadows of any individual,"[9] Judaism has been teaching precisely that for centuries. The theological underpinnings of the tradition's approach to leadership, namely that only God's reign is absolute, that human power must be circumscribed and shared, and that leaders are accountable to both God and the people, all stand in sharp contrast to the values inherent in the Great Man view of leadership.

Chief among Judaism's objections to the Great Man approach is that it perpetuates a view of the leader as flawless. The perfectionist model suggests that the leader can do anything and fix everything. He (and it was almost always he) is looked upon as a god, an infallible hero. When the leader is revealed to be less than perfect, as is inevitably the case, dreams are shattered, followers are traumatized, and the entire enterprise stands on the precipice of disaster.

Far more realistic is the traditional Jewish approach to the question of flawed leaders. As every religious school child has been taught, the Torah entertains no illusions about unblemished leadership. The dominant personalities of the Bible are richly contoured; none of them is one-dimensional. Not merely Scripture's most nefarious characters, but each of the biblical leaders is deeply flawed, a direct result of being human. Abraham endangered his wife's life to save his own reputation; Rebekah deceived her husband and son to advance her own agenda; Tamar seduced her father-in-law; Moses consistently battled both his temper and his ego; and David had a man killed in pursuit of his own sexual appetites. The differences between this approach and the perfectionism inherent in the Great Man Theory are striking. Without the pretense of flawlessness, leadership becomes the purview of the many, not the few. Since the leader is no more inherently virtuous than the followers, good leadership involves enabling and empowering, not commanding and controlling.

In Judaism, the idea of a perfect leader, other than God, is not only unrealistic, it is undesirable, as well. In a remarkable text, quoted in the name of Rabbi Simeon ben Jehozadak, a third-century CE sage living in the land of Israel, the rabbis of the Talmud actually expressed a preference for flawed leaders!

One should not appoint any one administrator of a community, unless he carries a
basket of reptiles on his back [something reprehensible in his background], so that
if he becomes arrogant, one could tell him, "Turn around."[10]

In contrast to what has become today's conventional expectation, that leaders
maintain a spotless and unimpeachable record, the Talmud articulates a radically different standard. Cognizance of weakness actually keeps leaders
"human." As the text suggests, it is difficult to lord power over others when
one's own shortcomings are a matter of public record. In the context of such
a perspective then, there is no reason to maintain a pretext of perfection
among those who lead.

The rabbis recognized that human weakness can be transformed into effective leadership. Presaging Flaubert, they refused to allow perfection to
become the enemy of the good. Inspired by the example of biblical leaders
such as King David, who, while punished for arrogance and inappropriate
manipulation of power, was not removed from leadership altogether, the rabbis knew that human frailty and failure are valuable components in the
growth and development of a leader. Here again, Judaism's early insights
continue to be corroborated by contemporary research into effective leadership. In study after study, successful leaders report the positive impact that
initial failures, including profound personal mistakes, have had on their ultimate maturation *as leaders*.[11]

In rejecting the Great Man Theory, contemporary approaches to effective
leadership have come to embrace another of Judaism's most important
insights; at the core of good leadership is the ability to identify, nurture, and
train the next generation of leaders. The expectation that a single individual
will magically arise with the knowledge, competency, and personality to lead
is naïve. Of necessity then, leadership development and succession planning
cannot be left to chance. Such work is not tangential to what a leader does; it
lies at the very heart of his or her effectiveness. Today's most successful leaders are fully devoted to nurturing and training those who will succeed them.
They recognize that the next generation must be carefully groomed in a process that can take years and requires a considerable outlay of resources.[12]

The wisdom of these teachings, notwithstanding, in much of the corporate
world, in politics, and all too often in the Jewish community, as well, vestiges
of the Great Man Theory persist. Even those who would otherwise repudiate
its more extreme elements continue to embrace the view that if only the one
right "hero" could be elected, recruited, or hired, all would be well; the enterprise would be protected. Because of a persistent belief that a single "great"

leader will simply come along to solve all the problems, the development of future leaders often receives short shrift from the very people who should be most concerned about it.

Difficult as it may be for long-serving leaders to plan beyond their own tenure, that is exactly what they must do. The Torah suggests that it was precisely this capacity that enabled Moses to become the truly great leader he was. In the Book of Numbers several examples of his deep-seated personal commitment to "replacing" himself are delineated. In the first instance, the text describes an elaborate process by which Moses's spirit was to be transferred to seventy elders of Israel in anticipation of a time when he would no longer serve as the singular head of the nation. Though the details of the story are obscured, it appears that two individuals, Eldad and Medad, sought to assume leadership of the people without following every aspect of the established procedure. Concerned that this made them somehow unsuitable to serve as leaders, "a youth ran out and told Moses, saying, 'Eldad and Medad are acting the prophet in the camp!'" At this news, Moses's loyal lieutenant (and eventual successor), Joshua, believing that Moses would be greatly displeased by this independent attempt to take over the reigns, proclaimed, "My lord Moses, restrain them!" Moses, however, was not at all troubled by Eldad and Medad's assertion of autonomous leadership. On the contrary, he understood that the real job of a great leader is to nurture and encourage leadership in others, whether or not it conforms to a preconceived conventional notion. "But Moses said to him, 'Are you wrought up on my account? Would that all the Lord's people were prophets, that the Lord put His spirit upon them!'"[13]

Unlike many, who appreciate the *theory* of leadership development without actually behaving accordingly, Moses was the kind of leader who understood the imperative of selecting and training others while there was still time to make a difference. Throughout his entire career he was dedicated to the empowerment of followers. He constantly adjusted his own leadership style in order to make room for the emergence of others. He knew when to intervene and when to fade into the background. He had the capacity to (in the words of the U.S. Army leadership training manual) "power down without powering off."[14] When finally he did learn that his leadership was coming to an end, his reaction was telling and unequivocal; he immediately beseeched God to name his successor. "Moses spoke to the Lord, saying, 'Let the Lord, Source of the breath of all flesh, appoint someone over the community who shall go out before them and come in before them, and who shall take them out and bring them in, so that the Lord's community may not be like sheep that have no shepherd.'"[15]

Far from a "logical" reaction, Moses's approach to this issue is counterintuitive. Having just been informed by God that his life's dream—entering the

Holy Land—would not be realized, Moses might have walked away in disgust and resentment. Surely, a lesser individual would have wrung his hands and concluded that the fate of the nation was now someone else's worry. Moses, however, understood that realizing personal goals is not the essence of great leadership. Disappointed as he surely must have been, Moses remained focused on the ultimate objective, taking the Jewish people safely to the Land of Israel. To make certain that this would happen, someone else would need to take over, and he knew that his job would not be complete unless and until he facilitated that transition. Moses's true testament then, is that he remained fixed on the need for continued leadership. In the end, it was not about him, about one Great Man. Rather, it was about developing the next generation of leaders who would continue to serve both God and the people.

Significantly, when it came time to recognize his successor, Joshua, Moses was neither bitter nor restrained. In fact, according to the rabbis, he went above and beyond what might have been expected in publicly empowering his protégé. When God tells Moses to move forward with the selection of Joshua, the text reads, "And the Lord answered Moses, 'Single out Joshua son of Nun, an inspired man, and lay your *hand* upon him'" (emphasis added).[16] Several verses later the text reads, "Moses did as the Lord commanded him . . . He laid his *hands* upon him and commissioned him . . ." (emphasis added).[17] To the sages, the difference between "hand" and "hands" was no mere editorial slip. As they saw it, Moses was only obligated to take a minimalist course of action, by laying one *hand* upon Joshua, and graciously stepping aside. In his view, however, the creation of new leaders was so important that he willingly exceeded the bare essentials, and, with "a full measure," did "more than he had been commanded." The use of both *hands,* then, is a metaphor that signals his enthusiastic endorsement of his successor. In so doing, Moses made Joshua a "full and heaped up vessel," a leader worthy of assuming Moses-like responsibility for the future of the Jewish people.[18] Moses thus demonstrates that a leader must not merely accord lip service or begrudging acquiescence to the idea of replacing himself. Only when his successor was firmly secured could he truly consider his job to be complete.

Such a perspective, however, ought not suggest that a continual effort to develop leaders will inevitably guarantee a uniform level of quality. In fact, the Torah makes it perfectly clear that leaders are not equally talented. When God agrees to Moses's request to name a successor, he instructs Moses to "invest him [Joshua] with *some* of your authority, so that the whole Israelite community may obey" (emphasis added).[19] Biblical commentators hastened to observe that the language of the text—"*some* of your authority"—is remarkably unambiguous.[20] It would have been impossible for the entirety of

Moses's greatness to be passed on to his successor, however well qualified. Leaders always come with a diversity of skills and talents. The goal of leadership development is not absolute replication. A leader's job is not to clone himself or herself. It is to develop the assets and abilities of those who can assume the mantle of leadership in the future.

Once again, the practical ramifications of these teachings are considerable. Despite traditional wisdom on the importance of leadership development, most contemporary synagogues and other Jewish not-for-profits approach the issue in a rather haphazard fashion, employing what might be called the "parachuting" method.[21] Here, prominent or wealthy individuals, often with little experience or training, are "dropped," or "parachuted" into positions of responsibility at the last minute. More often than not, this takes place at or near the end of an incumbent's term of office, with little or no advance planning. Because of a persistent belief that a single "great" leader will solve all the problems, few Jewish groups ever approach the question of volunteer or professional succession in a methodical and timely fashion.

As heirs to a great tradition, profoundly committed to the importance of nurturing and empowering the next generation of leaders, it is unfortunate that the organized Jewish community rarely takes a comprehensive approach to these issues. Even on those occasions when organizations and groups do offer courses or programs purporting to be leadership development, they are most often episodic and/or highly elitist. In their approaches, they tend to focus either on the development of management skills (e.g., budgeting, agenda planning, public relations) or general Jewish literacy (i.e., holidays, history, practices). While each of these areas may be important to the success of Jewish organizational life, none can legitimately be called leadership development. The lesson of Moses and subsequent Jewish authorities is that leadership cultivation is a comprehensive and pervasive mindset, not a course offering or occasional seminar. Unless leadership development is a goal of the entire enterprise, beginning with the current leaders, then all other efforts are destined to fall short.

Leadership succession planning must be on the agenda of every successful enterprise. Committees must have vice-chairs who, in the end, will prove more important than the chairperson. Organizations must seek constantly to identify and train promising individuals. Followers must be given meaningful opportunities to "practice" leadership, and credible individuals must be tapped for leadership even if they do not seem to fit the currently accepted mold.

Given Judaism's insistence that leadership is not the purview of an exclusive caste, and its equally passionate affirmation that even the best leader is flawed, it is critically important that programs claiming to be leadership development incorporate mentoring and coaching into the way they do business. Traditional teachings understand that leaders need partners for both counsel and comfort. It is not enough to drop someone into high office without a system of ongoing support. To be sure, mentoring and coaching in the organized Jewish community may engender considerable resistance on several fronts. As is true about sharing power, communal leaders are often reticent to seek advice from others, believing that such actions may reflect poorly upon their status and abilities. Rabbis are often uncomfortable divulging their weaknesses, particularly if lay people are involved. Wealthy philanthropists, accustomed to having all the answers in business, are sometimes embarrassed to be "coached" in their communal efforts. Young professionals feel vulnerable enough without exposing their need for further guidance.

Understandable as such concerns may be, they have no place in a leadership model that acknowledges human foibles as endemic to the process. What better example for today's Jewish leaders—lay and professional—than Moses being mentored by Jethro, his non-Jewish father-in-law (Exodus 18:14-24)? Relieved of the unrealistic expectations of the Great Man model, those who lead Jewish organizations need safe and nurturing venues in which to acknowledge, explore, and transcend their imperfections. The organized community then would do well to invest in mentoring and coaching opportunities as vital components of its approach to leadership training and continuing education. The development of effective leaders over the long term requires a willingness to move beyond the Great Man, not only in theory, but in practice, as well.

A final observation regarding leadership development in today's Jewish community. In many Jewish groups there is a tendency to pay lip service to traditional views on leadership by focusing attention exclusively upon the life and times of Moses as a role model for today's Jewish leaders. Oft-times this takes the form of a *d'var torah* (teaching) or sermonette at the start of a board meeting or in the context of a professional development conference. Ironically, this trend is not only naïve, it is terribly misleading. Where premodern Jewish authorities went out of their way *not* to apotheosize any human leader, even one as significant as Moses, today's Jewish groups have sought to reduce the complexity of Jewish writings on leadership to a few out-of-context verses, that in the aggregate often degenerate into nothing more than hero worship. Thus, for example, while the sages went out of their way to exclude Moses's name from the *haggadah* of Passover, lest anyone confuse his role with God's, today it has become standard operating procedure among many Jewish organizations to turn Moses into an "ideal type," the functional equivalent of Judaism's Great Man. Rarely do such discussions include any serious consideration of Moses's weaknesses as a leader and what can be learned from them. Moreover, they ignore the fact that, far from an easy-to-emulate leader, Moses's model is anomalous. As the only Jewish leader sanctioned by God to wear all three crowns of leadership simultaneously, he can never be cast as *the* quintessential Jewish leader.[22] Thus, to the degree that the case of Moses has something to teach today's Jewish leaders about leadership—and it most assuredly does, if approached seriously—such discussions must begin by recognizing his many imperfections, along with his strengths, as well as the fact that no subsequent Jewish leader should ever hope to replicate his model.

Because even the best leaders are transitory, not idolized Great Men, the health and vitality of an enterprise depend upon the continued development of the next generation. Those heads of contemporary Jewish organizations, lay and professional, inclined to see themselves in the tradition of Moses would do well to truly heed his example by placing much greater emphasis upon the development of new leaders in a thoughtful and planned fashion and far less attention upon the acquisition of personal goals, however noble and laudatory.

In repudiating the view of leadership typically associated with the Great Man ideal, Jewish sources (along with today's most respected theories from the general literature) do not devalue the importance of leadership altogether. Where the Great Man Theory is an example of biased attribution, unfairly exaggerating the influence of a single individual, Judaism recognizes that the reality is far more complex. While leadership can, in fact, be determinative on occasion, it is rarely the only variable in explaining the course of events. To be sure, insists the Talmud, a leader may exert substantive influence upon followers. "Woe to the ship whose captain has been lost," taught the rabbis.[23] And similarly, "When the shepherd is lost, so are the sheep."[24]

On the other hand, classical sources recognized that individual leaders are only one part of an elaborate and complex nexus of relevant factors that account for developments within an organization. In a compilation of legal and folkloristic commentaries on the Bible, the rabbis observed, "If there is no flock, what shall the shepherd do?"[25] Despite stereotypical portrayals of leaders as heroic figures single-handedly determining the fate of their enterprises, most serious students of leadership would acknowledge that this matter is far more nuanced. A hasidic teaching from Rabbi Moses of Kobryn (d. 1858) provides a charming, yet potent, insight.

The rabbi of Kobryn said: He who is a leader in Israel must not think that the Lord of the world chose him because he is a *great man*. If the king chose to hang his crown on a wooden peg in the wall, would the peg boast that its beauty drew the king's gaze to it (emphasis added)?[26]

Leaders may think of themselves as overwhelmingly important. But, Jewish leaders, accountable to both God and the people, must keep perspective and guard against inflating their own self-worth.

As if to synthesize this matter, the Talmud records a fascinating debate between Rabbi Yehudah Nesiah and his rabbinic colleagues on this very issue. "Rabbi Yehudah Nesiah and the rabbis disagreed. One said: According to the leader, so the generation. The other said: According to the generation, so the leader."[27]

More than merely a clever wordplay, this brief text highlights the intricacy associated with the question of leadership's ultimate importance. As is true in many rabbinic debates, the real lesson to be learned from this text lies not in the "or" but in the "and." The savvy student will understand that it is not Rabbi Yehudah's opinion *or* the rabbis'. Rather, the truth lies in the fact that both views, presented simultaneously, are equally correct. There are times when a single leader does, in fact, exert overarching influence, *and* there are countless other occasions when circumstances exercise a far greater impact than any single individual.

In spite of the popular tendency then to forever seek a "great" person as leader, Judaism has always preferred a different, and far more realistic, approach. While not refuting the impact one person can have, classical sources assert that leadership is not unique to a special class of select individuals alone. Developing and empowering the leadership potential of the next generation, therefore, is a critical component of every leader's work. Furthermore, Judaism acknowledges that all leaders, even the best, are, by definition, flawed. Not only is this a reality; in the long run, it is much better than clinging to a naïve expectation of perfectionism. Imperfect leaders have no reason to be arrogant and are less inclined to abuse their office or to behave imperiously.

In recent decades, contemporary experts have come to similar conclusions about leadership and have distanced themselves from the old Great Man Theory. As congregations and Jewish organizations seek to incorporate the best practices of leadership, culled from the most sophisticated research, perhaps they too will come to appreciate the wisdom of traditional Jewish teachings. Far more important for Jewish groups than the elusive pursuit of a single "great" leader are those efforts to consistently and continuously develop the leadership "greatness" of those within their ranks.

NOTES

1. R. M. Stogdill, "Personal Factors Associated with Leadership," *Journal of Psychology* no. 25 (1948): 35–71.

2. James MacGregor Burns, *Leadership* (New York: HarperCollins, 1978), 243–48.

3. Thomas Carlyle, *On Heroes, Hero-Worship and the Heroic in History* (Lincoln: University of Nebraska Press, 1966), 1.

4. J. C. Herold, ed., *The Mind of Napoleon: A Selection from His Written and Spoken Words* (New York: Columbia University Press, 1955), 289.

5. Warren G. Bennis and Robert J. Thomas, *Geeks and Geezers—How Era, Values, and Defining Moments Shape Leaders* (Boston: Harvard Business School Press, 2002), 82.

6. Gary Yukl, *Leadership in Organizations* (Upper Saddle River, NJ: Prentice Hall, 2002), 431–33.

7. Ronald A. Heifetz and Marty Linsky, *Leadership on the Line* (Boston: Harvard Business School Press, 2002), 123–39.

8. Bennis and Thomas, *Geeks and Geezers*, 83.

9. Bennis and Thomas, *Geeks and Geezers*, 159.

10. *Yoma* 22b.

11. See Bennis and Thomas on the "Crucibles of Leadership," *Geeks and Geezers*, 87–120.

12. General Electric's Jack Welch, for example, was selected to become chairman of the company only after more than nine years of careful training and analysis, according to Noel M. Tichy and Stratford Sherman's book, *Control Your Destiny or Someone Else Will* (New York: HarperCollins Publishers, 1993), 51. For additional information on the importance of leadership training and succession planning, see Jay A. Conger and Beth Benjamin, *Building Leaders—How Successful Companies Develop the Next Generation* (San Francisco: Jossey-Bass, 1990); and David Giber, Louis Carter, and Marshall Goldsmith, eds., *Best Practices in Leadership Development Handbook* (San Francisco: Jossey-Bass/Pfeiffer, 2000).

13. Numbers 11:24–29.

14. *Army Leadership—Be, Know, Do*, Field Manual No. 22–100 (Washington, DC, 1999), 1–13.

15. Numbers 27:15–17.

16. Numbers 27:18.

17. Numbers 27:22–23.

18. See Rashi and *Sifre* to Numbers 27:23.

19. Numbers 27:20.

20. See Rashi and *Sifre* to Numbers 27:20, and *Bava Batra* 75a.

21. Relevant information on the training of American Jewish leaders may be found in Gerald B. Bubis, ed., *The Director Had a Heart Attack and the President Resigned—Board-Staff Relations for the 21st Century* (Jerusalem: Jerusalem Center for Public Affairs, 1999). In particular, see the essay by Bubis, "Present Realities and Future Possibilities," 5–73; and the article by Bubis and Steven M. Cohen, "American Jewish Leaders View Board-Staff Relations," 87–131. Also see my article, "Making Leaders: How the American Jewish Community Prepares Its Lay Leaders," *Journal of Jewish Communal Service* 80, no. 2–3 (Summer/Fall 2004): 151–59.

22. For Moses as priest, see Leviticus 8:10–35. For Moses as prophet, see Deuteronomy 34:10. For Moses as sovereign, see Exodus 18:13–27.

23. *Bava Batra* 91b.

24. *Bava Kamma* 52a.

25. *Yalkut Bo* 187.

26. Cited in Martin Buber, *Tales of the Hasidim—Later Masters* (New York: Schocken Books, 1948), 167.

27. *Arachin* 17a.

Chapter Six

Of Competence and Character

If, as Judaism maintains, there is no singular, defining characteristic of leadership, and, if efficacy as a leader has more to do with *behavior* than with innate personality or physical appearance, then a precise understanding of the particular behaviors associated with successful leadership is essential for those with positions of responsibility in the Jewish community. The general literature on leadership often insinuates a distinction between leadership *skills*, those technical competencies a leader requires, and leadership *traits*, those personal attributes often thought to constitute the essence of good leadership.[1] Research on the subject reflects wide differences of opinion as to which of the two matters most.

In Jewish sources no such bifurcation exists. According to the Talmud, no one can be appointed a communal leader unless he or she is completely trustworthy; indeed, individuals "were not to exercise authority over the community, but that they were to be trusted."[2] Since followers trust their leaders only when they are assured both of their competence, that is, that they can get the job done, and of their integrity, a Jewish leader must possess both simultaneously and in equal quantities. The formula for Judaism's approach in this matter derives from the Torah itself. In a previously cited section of the Torah, Jethro stipulates the essential elements of effective leadership when he instructs his son-in-law, Moses, as follows: "You shall . . . seek out from among all the people *capable* men who *fear God* . . ."[3] With unambiguous eloquence, the priest from Midian thus synthesizes the two broad categories of effective leadership in Jewish thought: competence and character. Without both, effective leadership is elusive. Absent essential competencies, whether technical, interpersonal, or intellectual, no individual, however morally fit, will succeed as a leader. Similarly, even the most competent and skilled experts will fail to inspire the trust of their followers if they lack a moral grounding and ethical compass; if they are not what the tradition refers to as *yirei elohim*—God-fearing individuals. As USC's Warren Bennis is fond of saying, "It is not enough for a leader to do things right; he must do the right thing."[4] Thus, competence *and* character are essential for effective leadership.

COMPETENCE

While Jewish sources have a great deal to say about the requisite character attributes of leaders, delineating specific competencies is far more challenging. This is not because Judaism is any less committed to superior standards of performance. Rather, it reflects an understanding that the particular proficiencies required for effective leadership are not easily quantified. Indeed, the assumption, prevalent in some sectors of general leadership studies, that it is possible to construct a single, one-size-fits-all taxonomy of leadership skills that is fixed for all time is not supported in Jewish writings.

In the twelfth century, when Maimonides detailed the skill sets required by judges on the Sanhedrin, the national court, he stipulated:

> . . . only those are eligible to serve as members of the Sanhedrin . . . who are wise men and understanding, that is, who are experts in the Torah and versed in many other branches of learning; who possess some knowledge of the general sciences such as medicine, mathematics, (the calculation of) cycles and constellations; and somewhat acquainted with astrology, the arts of diviners, soothsayers, sorcerers, the superstitious practices of idolaters, and similar matters, so that they be competent to deal with cases requiring such knowledge.[5]

As Maimonides suggests, a leader is said to be competent only when he or she has the capacity to accurately assess the context of their work and the ability to access the knowledge necessary to accomplish the tasks at hand. The point is not that every leader must have the same base of knowledge or that leaders must know everything there is to know. It has long been observed, for example, that Jack Welch did not have to be an "expert on toaster manufacturing to make General Electric, a success," and Herb Kelleher did not have to "spend a lifetime flying airplanes to build Southwest Airlines."[6] Rather, leadership competency derives from possession of a specific base of technical knowledge and the ability to access and adapt information in rapidly changing situations and circumstances.

The absence in Judaism of a comprehensive immutable listing of aptitudes that every leader must have for all time reflects an understanding that proficiency in one arena does not automatically assure success in another. Talented congregational rabbis do not always make successful federation directors; esteemed scholars are not always the best pastors. In a system predicated upon shared and circumscribed power, the same leadership skills are not necessarily transferable from one *keter* to the next or interchangeable among milieux.[7] As far too many contemporary Jewish groups have learned the hard way, just because an individual proves adept as a business leader, for example, is no guarantee that she or he will succeed as a leader of a not-for-profit organization. It is a mistake to elevate people to positions of communal leadership simply because they have proven successful in other endeavors. Far more important than the acquisition of a singular set of proficiencies is a leader's capacity to inspire confidence and trust. Doing so requires a sophisticated understanding of the challenges at hand and the ability to respond to those challenges in an ever-changing environment. Only those individuals who are, as the Torah says, truly "capable," because they understand and are prepared for the context in which they must function, will be successful. As Bennis and Thomas found in their research on effective leaders:

> [T]raits and other factors are given far too much prominence in studies of leadership. Such factors rarely determine an individual's ultimate success . . . But more often, success, including the kind of success we label leadership, emerges as a result of an individual's ability to adapt to a crisis or challenge . . .[8]

Two other considerations contribute to a leader's competence, both of which are alluded to in the continuation of Maimonides' discussion of judges on the Sanhedrin.[9] The first is sincerity, the belief that a leader not only "talks the talk," but "walks the walk." Since sincerity, like motivation, is nearly impossible to assess objectively, in discussing this aspect of a leader's competency Maimonides emphasized only that which can be measured. He calls attention to the normally overlooked fact that a leader's sincerity is often evaluated by means that might be considered superficial or trivial but are, in fact, quite telling. "Every conceivable effort should be made to the end that all the members of that tribunal (the Sanhedrin) be of mature age, imposing stature, good appearance . . ." Significantly, Maimonides does not dismiss externalities, including the importance of a leader "looking the part." Rather, he acknowledged that trust is earned in a variety of ways, not all of which are linked to knowledge and skill sets. He gave expression to what followers understand intuitively but rarely articulate. When one holds office, certain behaviors "come with the territory," and conversely, others are deemed inappropriate for someone in that position. By any number of criteria, Maimonides argued, leaders must be perceived as apposite representatives of their enterprises, as appropriate embodiments of the very organizations they head. When leaders fail to "walk-the-walk," doubt is cast upon their overall competence; their ability to inspire trust is attenuated.[10]

In this regard, Maimonides reflected a perspective similar to that of the talmudic sages, though they expressed their views on the sincerity of leaders in decidedly more theocentric terms. To them, when a leader is duplicitous, saying one thing but doing another, or failing to live up to the tenets of the organization he or she leads, not only is personal effectiveness impeded, but such behavior actually causes embarrassment to God Himself.

> Israel's leaders put My own words to shame before the common people. How? A sage in the teacher's chair expounds in public "Thou shalt not lend money on interest," yet he himself lends his money on interest; "Thou shalt not rob," yet he himself robs; "Thou shalt not steal," yet he himself steals."[11]

A Jewish leader is a *dugma*—a role model—for followers. Thus, whether one is a synagogue trustee, a fund-raiser, an educator, or a philanthropist, certain behaviors can reasonably be expected to accompany the leadership experience. While the particulars vary from one post to another and may involve such things as participation in specific events, synagogue attendance, financial support, and the like, Jewish leaders cannot overlook the importance of behaving in ways that are consistent with the expectations of their office. Very often things that might be dismissed as superficial or unimportant are, in fact, essential to establishing trustworthiness for representatives of the community.

A final consideration mentioned by Maimonides in connection with a leader's competence is effective communication. Judges, he argued, "must be able to express their views in clear and well-chosen words, and be conversant with most of the spoken languages, in order that the Sanhedrin may dispense with the services of an interpreter." Simply put, it is difficult to assure followers of competence and trustworthiness if their leader cannot be understood or is perceived as ambiguous and abstruse. Despite their considerable diversity, every credible academic study of leadership concludes the same thing; namely that effective communication is "the central function of leadership."[12]

> Thus, whether in communicating his or her vision of the future to a large group of followers or in conducting his or her everyday and routine interactions with others, the leader is inescapably involved in the communicative processes . . .[13]

Importantly, Maimonides's point is not that only stirring orators or brilliant writers will succeed as leaders. To be sure, not every accomplished leader is eloquent; communication takes many forms. Nevertheless, a leader who cannot make himself or herself understood will rarely be considered competent by those whose trust needs to be secured.

CHARACTER

At the core of the Talmud's caveat that only those who are "to be trusted" can serve as community leaders, lies the pervasive issue of character. Notwithstanding the diversity of competencies required by the ketaric rubric (in which power is divided amongst and between three distinct paradigms of leadership), Judaism insists that all communal leaders—political, spiritual, and educational—should strive to achieve the highest level of moral excellence possible. Precisely because the tradition understands that power is inherently corrupting, it requires those who exercise it to be of unimpeachable repute. Community leaders are God's representatives, serving with the imprimatur of the people at large. In such a system, turpitude is not only bad ethics, it is bad business.

The obligation to serve as an ethical exemplar is not limited to so-called religious leaders alone. In this regard, the crown of sovereignty is no different from the crowns of torah or priesthood. Superlative character is as critical for a fund-raiser as for a rabbi. "Timeless leadership," argues Warren Bennis, "is always about character."[14] Classical Jewish sources insist that all those charged with responsibility for leading a community, regardless of portfolio, are likened to judges.[15] Not only are they entitled to the esteem accorded a judge;[16] they must be of similarly impeccable character, as well. "The elders of the community, who are appointed to deal with public or private matters are viewed as judges, and he who is disqualified from judging because of wrong-doing cannot be appointed to sit among them."[17] Improprieties, moral equivalence, and ethical defects matter in leadership. They cannot be ignored, discounted, or offset, regardless of how impressive one's skills are, how much Torah one knows, or how much money one contributes.

In discussing the question of character, Jewish authorities are especially concerned about the influence of money, both when it comes to recruiting leaders and once individuals are in office. The tradition recognizes and decries the tendency to appoint people to leadership based strictly upon their wealth.

Rabbi Mana cursed those who were appointed [in exchange] for payment of money. Rabbi Immi recited [the following verse] in their regard: "[You shall not make to be with Me] gods of silver, nor gods of gold shall you make for yourselves" (Ex. 20:20). Said Rabbi Josiah, "And the cloak that [such a person] wears [as a symbol of office] is like [nothing else than] the covering of an ass." Rav said, "This one who is appointed [in exchange] for a payment of money: they do not rise before him and they do not call him 'Rabbi;' the cloak that he wears is like [nothing else than] the covering of an ass." Rabbi Zeira and one of the rabbis were in session. One of those who had been appointed in exchange for a payment of money happened to pass by. Said one of the rabbis to Rabbi Zeira, "Let us show ourselves to be repeating traditions, and not rise up before him."[18]

This disdain for those who "buy" their way into office continues throughout Jewish writings, even to the present era, without regard to the type of leader in question. Simply put, anyone—learned rabbi or layperson—who came into office based on wealth alone was suspect and subject to insult and affront. In the Middle Ages, Maimonides castigated his own rabbinical colleagues for deriving "temporal advantage from the words of the Torah."[19] Across Europe, communal rabbis were routinely attacked for placing their personal economic interests above the will of God and the needs of the people. In the words of the late-sixteenth-, early-seventeenth-century rabbi, Ephraim Luntshitz:

> So many rabbis are unwilling to raise their voices in vehement protest against the iniquities of their time lest in so doing they jeopardize the chance of promotion to the more prominent positions of the land. Others, not quite so ambitious in their designs, studiously refrain from combating the forces of evil lest they give offence and imperil their popularity with the people. They will rather protect their own honor than promote God's glory.[20]

So too, the early hasidic leader, Rabbi Yaakov Yosef, accused "rabbis . . . whose livelihood comes to them from the people of the community and its leaders" of excessive obsequiousness and of doing whatever it takes to gain favor with the wealthy.[21] He likened these rabbis to those who built the golden calf. Just as the Israelites wanted a god "who shall go before us" (Exodus 32:1), so "nowadays the cities are full of rabbis 'who go before us' and lust after power . . ."[22] Obsessed with their own material needs, rabbis lacked the courage and backbone to stand up for what was right. In what is surely the harshest of judgments, Yaakov Yosef denounces their misuse of power as a form of adultery. "Just as the unfaithful wife who, in the very moment when she lies with her husband, thinks of the lewdness of her adulteries, so it is with the learned who, while they study the Torah, commit adultery with the wealthy members of the community."[23]

Medieval lay leaders, whose only claim to power was their wealth, were ridiculed, as well. In the following example, drawn from the writings of the fourteenth-century rabbi, Kalonymus ben Kalonymus, the arrogance and sense of entitlement of the well-heeled laity are mocked. Pretending to speak as one of them, Kalonymus writes:

> There is none other than me. I decide yes or no. With my own strength I made this city in which the people now dwell. I preserved it . . . I weigh money into the Emperor's coffers like precious jewels. And money will answer everything . . . Can one

who has no money defer an evil decree? And can he who does not have the where-withal close the breach?[24]

Similar concerns are evidenced in modernity too. In nineteenth-century Russia, for example, certain individuals who were appointed by the government and dubbed "crown rabbis" (*rabbanim mi-taam* in Hebrew) were derisively dismissed by their coreligionists as nothing more than paid stooges for the government.[25] Even in America, established rabbis, communal professionals, and philanthropists are regularly accused of placing a price tag on Jewish life, caring more about money than God and spirituality, and preferring an oligarchic system in which the "golden rule"—the one who has the gold rules—is the regnant precept. In explaining why he believes so many contemporary young American Jews walked away from Judaism, Jewish Renewal leader Rabbi Michael Lerner notes the following:

> The Jewish world that they encountered seemed to be obsessed with money and power . . . Inside the synagogues, and even more so in the major communal organizations of Jewish life—like the United Jewish Appeal or Jewish Federation, but also including the American Jewish Committee, Hadassah, B'nai B'rith—the people who had the most power and money had the most influence. Everyone intuitively understood this: that what really counted was how much money you had and how much you could give, or alternatively how well you did at being a fundraiser and getting others to give.[26]

Despite their diversity, Jewish writings seem to display a remarkable consistency on this matter: those whose office derives strictly from wealth rarely make good leaders. Related to this issue is the concern that once in power, individuals are especially susceptible to the allure of money, either in the form of bribery or other illicit enticements. As the prophet Micah makes clear, this is no mere coincidence. Leaders of the community are particularly vulnerable.

> Hear this, I pray you, you heads of the house of Jacob, and rulers of the house of Israel, that abhor justice, and pervert all equity; that build up Zion with blood, and Jerusalem with iniquity. The heads thereof judge for reward, and the priests thereof teach for hire, and the prophets thereof divine for money.[27]

To protect against these abuses, the Torah cautioned against appointing anyone who might be seduced by ill-gotten gains.[28] Rabbinic commentators understood this command in different ways; some held that only those who cannot be sued in a court of law because of finances are eligible for high office, others interpreted it to mean that leaders should despise money altogether, while still others insisted that a leader must reject all monetary compensation entirely.[29] In every case, the biblical exegetes recognized the danger that money can have to a leader's credibility, impartiality, and general reputation. Indeed, Maimonides made the argument that judges who "hate money" are far more desirable than any others.[30] As a general precept, Jewish sources hold that no matter how competent a leader may be, when money and authority are mixed together, "the eyes of the wise are blinded" and "just words become crooked."[31] For all these reasons, temptations must be removed, and every effort must be instituted to eliminate even the appearance of errant activity.

The intensity of these writings on the subject of money and leadership must be evaluated carefully. To state clearly what may seem a subtle point, the very fact that so much material exists on this subject indicates that, despite all the protestations and caveats, wealth has always been a critical factor in communal leadership. According to the historian Salo Baron, even in Greco-Roman times Jewish communities were run as oligarchies in which wealthy individuals exercised disproportionate control over communal policies.

> There is little doubt that . . . wealth counted heavily in selecting leaders and influencing communal action. In those fairly numerous cases in which individual members endowed a synagogue with all or a major part of the funds necessary for construction or maintenance, the donor's voice undoubtedly was loudly heard in council.[32]

Not only was this true in any given generation, but ancient practices of hereditary inheritance guaranteed that the same wealthy families continued to rule for many years to come.

So, too, in the Middle Ages, where affluent *parnasim* controlled the community councils and regional "supercommunal" organizations that were responsible for the internal self-government of the Jewish communities. For all of the concerns about character then, an unmistakable affinity between wealth and community leadership seemed to dominate Jewish communal life in the period.

The necessity of raising a sufficient tax base certainly made such an alliance logical. In medieval Europe, Jewish communities were expected to provide enough funds, in the form of taxes, to satisfy an expansive array of demands from Gentile authorities (the Church, feudal landowners, the caliphate, etc.). In addition, Jews were responsible for generating the money necessary to support their own infrastructures, which often included schools, synagogues, personnel (rabbis, teachers, ritual slaughterers, beadles, etc.), charitable organizations, and the like. While systems for tax assessment and collection varied from one community to another, not surprisingly, the wealthy were often looked to by their less fortunate coreligionists to provide sizeable percentages of these revenues.[33] For this reason, affluent individuals had a vested interest in overseeing the tax processes and assumed a significant role in governing their community. Not coincidentally, these same individuals were the only people who could afford the leisure time and extra financial obligations required of communal service.[34] Where most of the population was preoccupied simply trying to make a living, only the well to do were in a position to become leaders with all of its extra demands.

Further, wealthy Jews were uniquely suited to lead their communities in negotiating the tempestuous waters of relations with non-Jews. Such individuals were usually in the best position to access the halls of power, to make presentable and respectable appearances, to speak the local language, and to provide bishops, kings, and landowners with what they wanted, usually additional monies. In return, they were sometimes able to buy favorable consideration for themselves and their community. Over the centuries, a diversity of leadership posts, known by a variety of titles, including *shtadlan* (intercessor), *nagid*, court Jew, and Chief "Rabbi," among others, arose for these and related purposes. To their great credit, such leaders were sometimes able to negotiate special protection, including reduced tax burdens and extended permission to remain in residence, thus improving, even temporarily, Jewish life in the Middle Ages.

While realities changed, many of the links between wealth and leadership that appeared in premodern communities continued *mutatis mutandis* into modernity in areas ranging from revenue generation to interfaith relations to political advocacy. By the nineteenth century, though Jews were no longer *imperium in imperio*, a nation within a nation, and though an independent system of self-imposed, compulsory taxation ceased to exist, Jews maintained elaborate structures of religious, educational, and social agencies run by and for the Jewish community. Even in those cases in Europe when government funding was available, the need for Jewish communities to generate sizeable amounts of additional monies continued unabated. Once again, it was the wealthy who stepped forward and to them that prominent leadership posts were awarded.

Throughout modernity, Jewish communities the world over have achieved great things, thanks in large measure to the leadership of wealthy individuals who were willing to put up the money and dedicate their efforts to Jewish causes. Synagogues and recreation facilities, academic institutions and absorption centers, camps and soup kitchens . . . The list is endless. Many of the most notable accomplishments of Jewish life in the twentieth century from Zionism and the State of Israel to day schools and university Jewish Studies programs owe much to the leadership of the affluent.

Notwithstanding all of the concerns about wealthy individuals becoming communal leaders then, the historical record suggests that this issue is painted in many more shades of gray than might be thought. Indeed, despite the preponderance of material to the contrary, some traditional sources actually suggest that linking leadership to money can, in fact, be a good thing. In his commentary on the previously examined section of Exodus, when Jethro first advised Moses to appoint "capable men who fear God," the eleventh-century exegete Rabbi Solomon ben Isaac (Rashi) offers a unique perspective. In explicating the Torah's requirement that leaders be *anshei hayil*—capable individuals—Rashi notes that the text is actually describing, "rich men, who will not need to flatter or to show favor."[35] In this view, wealth is not only *not* an impediment to leadership, it provides a distinct moral advantage. Those whose independent wealth makes it unlikely that they will derive any meaningful economic advantage from their communal efforts, may, in fact, be in the best position to exercise the most effective leadership of all. To Rashi, the prophylaxis of choice against bribery and ill-gotten gain is to appoint leaders who are sufficiently wealthy that they simply cannot be enticed.

A related argument in favor of wealthy leaders is mounted by another highly unlikely source, Rabbi Judah the Pious, author of the twelfth-century German mystical work *Sefer Hasidim* (The Book of the Pious). Despite the fact that Rabbi Judah was highly critical of the established Jewish community of his day, he appeared to recognize that, when coupled with learning and piety, affluence made for particularly effective communal leadership. Since then (as now), prosperous individuals often had the freedom to do what they wanted and the influence necessary to get things accomplished, Rabbi Judah believed that a leader's possession of wealth was actually an efficacious means of serving God. ". . . when you have rich Sages who are guides and who are filled with erudition of Torah learning and who are wealthy besides, then they are heeded . . ."[36]

An honest reading of all these sources, then, suggests that questions about the role of wealth in communal leadership deserve much greater consideration than they customarily receive. While not unique to the American Jewish community, it is certainly the case that Jewish organizations and institutions rarely devote serious attention to the character of their leaders and to the role that money plays in both their rise to power and the conduct of their work. On the one hand, these writings leave little doubt that wealth has always had a prominent place in the appointment of Jewish communal leaders. Indeed, the realities of Jewish history, premodern and contemporary, have made the ability to generate considerable funds, either in the form of taxes or philanthropy, nothing short of a core competency for many in positions of communal responsibility. Not surprisingly, the individuals who are the source of those funds have more than a passing interest in their disposition. The Hebrew expression *baal hamea, hu baal hadea*—"the master of the grain is the master of the idea"—says it all. Only the most naïve would seek to deny such affinities. Moreover, throughout history, there are numerous instances in which affluence, far from being a necessary "evil" in leadership, has actually proven to be a distinct advantage for those in power, enhancing their overall impact and improving the lives of their followers.

On the other hand, these classical texts insist that the possession of wealth is rarely a sufficient reason to elevate someone to leadership. That "money talks" is undeniable in Jewish history. That wealth automatically makes great leaders is as fallacious a notion as it is one widely held. In their collective wisdom, Jewish sources sound a cautionary note. No leader can succeed without engendering and sustaining the trust of followers. When doubts are raised about a leader's character, as inevitably occurs when one is perceived as buying office, long-term efficacy is compromised.

Moreover, regardless of how someone achieves high office, once there, the ability to withstand the enticements of riches and avoid the pitfalls of fiscal improprieties lies at the core of their success. This goes far beyond maintaining acceptable accounting practices or complying with requisite regulations. When a community leader's impartiality is cast into doubt because the special interests of the wealthy always seem to trump fairness and equity, the Talmud's basic criterion of trustworthiness is no longer met; a leader's ability to function is destroyed.

In a world in which financial scandals, bribery, and influence peddling are par for a leader's course (even religious and philanthropic leaders), Judaism's insistence that character matters represents a much-needed antidote to conventional practices. Minimizing the importance of such sensibilities will only imperil a leader's ability to inspire the trust necessary to function effectively. As the legatees of such insights, Jewish communities must lead the way in this regard. Critical as money has always been and will remain to the success of Jewish communal ventures, those who hold titled positions in the Jewish world ought to be thinking at least as much about character issues as about financial resource development.

Organizational nominating committees err grievously when they ignore the character of those being considered in favor of their ability to give and raise money. Lay and professional officers of Jewish groups, including congregational rabbis, do not enhance their own credibility or that of their enterprises if they are continuously perceived as kowtowing to the superrich. Wealthy philanthropists can hardly be said to be engaging in community building if their modi operandi ignore the needs, perspectives, and priorities of all but their affluent compatriots. Those responsible for educating and preparing Jewish professional leaders—from JCC directors to congregational rabbis—must also begin to consider the matter of character and leadership. Particularly for those whose livelihood depends on it, learning how to balance the best interests of the community-at-large and the agenda of the wealthy whose ongoing support remains vital, ought to be an essential part of the training process.

While, for good reason, Jewish authorities focused considerable attention on the role of money in leadership, the tradition identifies a number of other issues that are similarly critical to a leader's integrity. High atop this list is the imperative that communal officers take personal responsibility for their own behavior. In the Torah this is dramatically depicted by the case of the Israelite priest (*kohen*) represented by the person of Aaron. In ancient Israel the *kohen* was charged with making atonement for the entire Jewish people, a weighty and awe-inspiring task to be sure. Because the Torah insists that, above all else, leaders must lead, Aaron is proscribed from offering the necessary sacrifices ("sin offerings") for the people-at-large until after he enters the "tent of meeting" by himself, stands before God, and confesses his own sins.[37] This confession is the necessary precursor to his work on behalf of the people. The Torah's message is quite clear; at the core of a leader's integrity is the obligation to acknowledge one's own shortcomings and to take full responsibility for them. Only after the requisite adjustments and compensations have been made can attention be turned to the work at hand; only then can an individual hope to engender the trust and moral persuasiveness necessary to lead effectively.

Among the academic experts who have written extensively in support of such a view are Harvard University's Ronald Heifetz and Marty Linsky. Though their language and frame of reference are decidedly secular, their tone and conclusions are consistent with the Torah's teachings. In a section of their book *Leadership on the Line*, headed "Accept Responsibility for Your Piece of the Mess," they write:

> When you belong to the organization or community that you are trying to lead, you are part of the problem. This is particularly true when you have been a member of the group for some time, as in a family. Taking the initiative to address the issue does not relieve you of your share of responsibility . . . In short, you need to identify and accept responsibility for your contributions to the current situation, even as you try to move your people to a different, better place . . . When you are too quick to

lay blame on others, whether inside or outside the community, you create risks for yourself.[38]

Related to this issue is the highly controversial question, particularly popular in recent years, of whether or not a leader is obligated to admit mistakes publicly. In some circles, there is a notion that doing so will compromise a leader's current or future value. Judaism, however, takes the polar opposite position, arguing emphatically that a leader is not only obligated to admit mistakes and offer a public apology but that doing so actually improves one's effectiveness as a leader.[39] (Readers will recall a talmudic text cited in the previous chapter suggesting that human foibles, represented metaphorically by "a basket of reptiles" on one's back, are also deemed an asset to leadership, not a liability.)

Since, according to the Bible, "there is no man who does not sin," leaders are under no obligation to pretend otherwise.[40] They, as everyone else, are required to confess and repent their transgressions. Even the most righteous leaders of all, known in Hebrew as the *tzaddikim*, are duty bound to admit their mistakes and seek forgiveness. According to a hasidic teaching, "In these generations all *tzaddikim* require repentance, because each has a flaw in himself to repair."[41] What continues to be hotly debated in many corporate and political arenas is simply indisputable in Jewish sources. Character matters in leadership, and as a result, leaders must apologize for their own mistakes and seek to make amends. Doing so neither diminishes their impact nor weakens their effectiveness.

To those who might argue that such a noble and lofty attitude is appropriate in the case of religious leaders but has no place in the "real" world, the Torah takes notable exception. After first detailing the procedures to be used for expiation of sins by the priests and then the general population, the Torah turns its attention to the military, economic, and political realm (*keter malkhut*):

> In case it is a chieftain (*nasi*) who incurs guilt by doing unwittingly any of the things which by the commandment of the Lord his God ought not to be done, and he realizes his guilt, or the sin of which he is guilty is brought to his knowledge, he shall bring as his offering a male goat without blemish. He shall lay his hand upon the goat's head . . .[42]

The text goes on to describe the appropriate sacrificial processes that, in the biblical world, constituted the functional equivalent of a public admission of wrongdoing. Thus, the Torah is quite clear. Leaders, whether they are "religious" or "secular," have an equal obligation to admit their mistakes.

Commenting on these verses, the first-century CE sage Rabbi Johannan ben Zakkai added an insight.

"In case it is a chieftain . . ." Rabbi Johannan ben Zakkai said: Happy is the generation whose ruler brings a sacrifice for a sin he has committed unwittingly. If its ruler
brings a sacrifice is there any need to say what one of the common people would do,
and if he brings a sacrifice for a sin he has committed unwittingly, is there any need
to say what he would do in case of a sin committed willfully?[43]

Rabbi Johannan understood that the public pays careful attention to its
leaders; their behavior serves as a powerful example. Those who refuse to
own up to their errors are sending a potent message to their followers. Conversely, when a leader who could easily shift responsibility for mistakes to
others nevertheless acknowledges personal wrongdoing and seeks public forgiveness, he or she has made an enormously important statement, one that
sets a tone and resonates throughout the polity.

Beyond admitting mistakes, a leader who wishes to inspire the trust of followers must, with consistency, tell the truth and fulfill his or her promises.
According to Maimonides, "One must not say one thing and mean another,
but like heart like face; we should express in words of mouth only what we
have in mind."[44] While such a principle may seem too obvious to even merit
mention, it stands in sharp contrast to what has come to be viewed as "standard operating procedure" for many of today's leaders. More often than not,
those who hold high office behave as if they have been given special dispen-
sation to make vain promises, knowing full well that they will not be held
accountable. Jewish sources stand resolutely opposed to such an attitude.
This point was underscored in an important 1967 decision of the Rabbinical
High Court in Israel in a case involving a government official who made a
promise while running for office and then reneged after the election. The ruling, which reflects millennia of Jewish teachings on the subject, notes that
even if a prominent official might legally argue (on the basis of a technicality)
that he is exempted from keeping a promise, the very fact that he is a leader
nullifies any such immunity. In the words of the court:

In conclusion, we must add and say . . . that as public servants, and when acting in
this capacity, they should not argue that the obligations which they undertook are
not binding because their validity can be disputed under law. Promises and obligations, especially in communal affairs, are holy and must be fulfilled to capacity, in
accordance with their original intent, wording and spirit. Public servants shall not
go back on their word and bring ruin on the public . . .[45]

Judaism's insistence on honesty in leadership means not only that a leader
must not lie; it means that effective leaders must tell the truth, even on those
occasions when the information being conveyed is difficult to take, painful,
or contrary to conventional wisdom. Indeed, the very essence of a leader's
work involves challenging followers to confront reality honestly and then

helping them to adapt to the inevitability of change. This should be as true in education and religion as it is in business and politics.[46] An individual unable to face reality with candor, and inspire others to do the same, may be an excellent manager but will never be an effective leader.[47]

Maintaining the organizational status quo, even when done with efficiency and finesse, is not leadership; nor is conflict-reduction for its own sake or the perennial pursuit of consensus simply because it is a less contentious option than airing honest differences of opinion. Long-standing loyalties, deeply entrenched practices, and political correctness must not be allowed to obfuscate the truth. Leaders must be honest enough to assess their own realities, those of the enterprise they head, and those of the world around them. Individuals who would rather be loved than honest and who prefer scapegoating to accountability are deceiving themselves and their followers. In today's Jewish world, lay leaders, agency directors, rabbis, and educators who fail to honestly confront the rapidly changing environment in which they work will suddenly find themselves and their institutions increasingly irrelevant in the lives of the very Jews they wish to engage. Being a leader is not the same as being a bureaucrat. A leader must be sufficiently honest to look in the mirror, to *become* that mirror for others, and to inspire candid organizational introspection on an ongoing basis.

The idea of continual self-examination is woven throughout the tapestry of Jewish sources. There is a well-known teaching in the Talmud that one is obligated to repent the day before death.[48] Since one never knows that precise time, the rabbis' message is that repentance must, of necessity, be an ongoing process. To facilitate meaningful repentance, many notable Jewish authorities insisted that one take a careful inventory of personal behavior on a daily basis.[49] Arguably, the principles that make this an effective way to lead one's life also make it an apt way to lead an organization. In other words, if being serious about personal *teshuvah* (repentance) means adopting an ongoing commitment to honest self-evaluation, the same must hold true in the institutions and organizations of the Jewish community. Communal leaders do themselves and their followers a disservice by failing to honestly analyze their organization's strengths and weaknesses with regularity. Exaggerating successes, minimizing challenges, and misrepresenting reality all in the name of institutional hype, marketing, or an unwillingness to rock the boat is not leadership.

In every generation, effective Jewish leaders helped their followers to look at themselves and their community realistically and with candor, challenging them to respond to new truths and the certainty of change. Beginning with Abraham, whose honesty inspired his followers to literally walk away from the conventional theology and practice of their day, great Jewish leaders have understood that effective leadership means telling the truth, even when doing so requires swimming against the tide of popular thought.

Bucking prevailing trends and helping followers to uncover essential and overarching truths epitomizes the leadership style of Moses. For him, as for all leaders, speaking the truth was filled with considerable risk, and the biblical narrative makes it clear that he did not always do it well. But, when he did, he was willing to challenge his own people, the Pharaoh, and even God, Himself. In the aftermath of the incident with the Golden Calf, for example, only Moses had the fortitude to "tell it like it is," to rout out the most egregious violators of God's commands and then to hold a mirror to the collective masses without any pretense or soft sell. "The next day Moses said to the people, 'You have been guilty of a great sin.' "[50]

Moses's goal, however, was not merely to chastise. Once having spoken the truth, a leader must guide followers through the difficult processes of radical change that follow. Moses understood that the only way the fissiparous Israelites would begin to adapt to new realities was when they came face to face with the truth about their own behaviors. As the leader, it was his job to articulate this point, however unpopular. It could not, however, be his last word on the subject. His excoriation was followed immediately (as the verse continues) by the assurance of a nurturing leader, "Yet I will now go up to the Lord; perhaps I may win forgiveness for your sin." Thus, Moses not only spoke the truth about the realities he and his people were facing, but he laid the groundwork for helping them to cope with the difficult changes still ahead.

Successful leaders must be willing to tell the truth to superiors as well as subordinates. The same honesty that made Moses effective with his followers also informed the way he dealt with God. Very much in the tradition of Abraham, whose own candid disputation with the Lord over the future of Sodom and Gomorrah (Genesis 18:23–32) solidified his position as a preeminent Jewish leader, Moses was willing to take on God when circumstances so mandated. Disgusted with the Israelites' excessively negative reaction following the report of the spies (who were sent to scout out the land of Canaan), God threatened to "disown" the Jewish people and start over with a new nation. Moses, however, refused to accept these realities uncritically. As the leader, he was obligated to force even God to confront the truth about these threatened actions. In strong and unadulterated language, he held a mirror directly to Him.

But Moses said to the Lord, "When the Egyptians, from whose midst You brought up this people in Your might, hear the news, they will tell it to the inhabitants of that land. Now they have heard that You, O Lord, are in the midst of this people; that

You, O Lord, appear in plain sight . . . If then You slay this people to a man, the nations who have heard Your fame will say, 'It must be because the Lord was power-less to bring that people into the land He had promised them on oath that He slaugh-tered them in the wilderness.' Therefore, I pray, let my Lord's forbearance be great . . ."[51]

Moses understood that a leader's duty to tell the truth applies at every level of the organizational chart. Loyal as he was, he could not have remained silent and continued as an effective leader.

Moses's example set the tone for an entire genre of subsequent Jewish leaders, the biblical prophets, of whom he is reported to have been the great-est.[52] More than any of the other *ketarim*, the prophets (*keter torah*) embodied this idea that a leader is obligated to speak with unbridled honesty, even if doing so arouses the ire of constituents. Implicit in many of the prophetic writings is an understanding that an individual who merely parrots the pre-vailing sentiment is no leader. The very act of leadership involves an uncom-promising commitment to forthrightness and change.

In strikingly harsh language and fearless tones, these "agents of change" criticized those who needed to hear the truth, from priests and kings to the people-at-large.[53] They highlighted the disastrous consequences that would surely follow absent radical shifts in behavior and attitude.[54] They took on the sacred beliefs of their day, separated fact from fiction, unmasked popular notions, and always sought to redirect the people's energies to what would truly bring them happiness and success. The prophets were anything but bureaucratic hacks who mindlessly echoed the company line. Their role as leaders meant that they were obligated to challenge even the most treasured of beliefs and practices.

Thus said the Lord of Hosts, the God of Israel: Add your burnt offerings to your other sacrifices and eat the meat! For when I freed your fathers from the land of Egypt, I did not speak with them or command them concerning burnt offerings or sacrifice. But this is what I commanded them: Do My bidding, that I may be your God and you may be My people; walk only in the way that I enjoin upon you; that it may go well with you."[55]

The Talmud describes a curious requirement associated with prophecy that has important ramifications for those in contemporary positions of communal leadership. According to the sages, one of the telltale signs of a "false" prophet is the lack of originality in the message being delivered. This seems rather unusual in view of the fact that prophets were supposed to be God's spokespeople, literally conveying the divine word, not creative writers. Nev-ertheless, the rabbis insisted that, "The same communication is revealed to many prophets, yet no two prophets prophesy in the identical phraseology."

They go on to note that on those occasions when multiple "prophets employed [exactly] the same expression, it proved that they said nothing."[56]

The point, according to the rabbis, is that effective leaders must be their own people. Those who follow the crowd, who merely mimic the conventional wisdom, are not leaders. They lack personal authenticity and will quickly be exposed as fraudulent. A successful leader, argues Warren Bennis, must have a "distinctive voice."[57] To be effective, leaders must find that voice and be willing to express it, even when doing so places them at odds with the majority. In Jewish law, if two or more witnesses in a court use precisely the same language to describe an alleged crime, their testimony is automatically suspected of being fabricated.[58] Similarly, judges are cautioned specifically *not* to follow the majority "to do evil."[59] While legal authorities have interpreted this instruction in a variety of ways, its simple meaning is clear; community leaders cannot allow themselves to be swept up and persuaded by conventional wisdom or the prevailing Zeitgeist. Leaders must hearken to their own voice and follow their own heart, regardless of how much pressure they face or how unpopular their decisions.

In the contemporary Jewish community considerable influence is often exerted on lay and professional officeholders to conform, to "go along in order to get along." Those who resist or who challenge these "sacred" assumptions are often criticized and isolated. Very often, the system rewards homogenization and discourages the development of a distinctive voice. In this regard, rabbinic teachings on false prophecy are particularly poignant. The sign of a true leader is the ability to reflect one's own authenticity, not to follow the majority blindly. The Talmud teaches that despite being created by the same God, every human being is unique.[60] A leader is obligated to live up to that uniqueness. Otherwise, like false prophets, such individuals may talk a great deal, but, in truth, they will have "said nothing."

Speaking the truth, however, is only the first step. Despite the ferocity of their message, the prophets, following the example of Moses, understood that real leadership requires something more than the unvarnished truth. It is one thing to "tell it like it is," without mincing words; anyone can level criticism. Leadership requires that followers be supported, guided, and empowered to transform themselves and their enterprise. It is absolutely true that "to be a prophet means to challenge," but effective leadership requires more. As Abraham Heschel observed about the prophets in his groundbreaking survey of their work, "every prediction of disaster is in itself an exhortation to repentance . . . Almost every prophet brings consolation, promise and the hope of reconciliation along with censure and castigation. He begins with a *message of doom*; he concludes with a *message of hope*."[61]

As is true of all Jewish leaders, the biblical prophets functioned within the context of a larger and more extensive system of shared and circumscribed power. Unlike many would-be leaders in today's Jewish community, however, they understood that it was not enough to criticize from the sidelines and then walk away. The prophets recognized the imperative for leaders to control the level of followers' stress by adjusting their own words and behaviors accordingly.[62] Their uncompromising honesty and harsh judgments did not prevent them from providing the support necessary for followers to adapt to a radically changed situation. Their leadership allowed the Jewish people to survive the destruction of Jerusalem, and subsequent exile from the land, without completely abandoning all hope. Their vision of a better future in which God had not completely turned away from the nation, in which as Isaiah predicted (10:21), "a remnant of Jacob shall return," serves as a model of leadership for future generations.

Since that time, effective Jewish leaders have, in fact, sought to emulate this approach, speaking the truth about current realities while offering the guidance necessary to effectuate appropriate change. Doing so seems no less relevant today when the discontinuous changes of contemporary Jewish life make both honest assessment and wise strategies for coping with them nothing less than essential.

When it comes to identifying, recruiting, and training its leaders, the contemporary Jewish community would do well to follow the tenets of classical Jewish sources by seeking individuals who are men and women of both competence and character. Recent survey research data suggest that fewer than half of all American Jews are affiliated with a synagogue, and even fewer are members of other Jewish organizations.[63] While such low rates of affiliation can hardly be blamed entirely on the efficacy of institutional leadership, it is worth considering how different things might be in a Jewish community where leaders reflect these twin standards of competence and character with consistency.

To be sure, many Jewish groups, past and present, proudly claim professional and volunteer leaders, who do, in fact, embody the Torah's ideal of "capable individuals who fear God." As such, these organizations more than meet the sages' criterion of only having "trusted" people appointed to "exercise authority over the community." The effectiveness and successes these individuals bring to their communities serve to underscore the wisdom of the tradition's insistence on both character and competence for all who aspire to wear the mantle of Jewish leadership. To the extent that a critique of the contemporary Jewish community is in order, the intent is not to overlook the existence of such men and women. Rather, their examples must serve as the standard, not the exception.

There is much to be gained by translating the tradition's ideal into reality at every level of the organized Jewish community. Serious thought must be given to the competencies required for each leadership post within an enterprise. Expectations must be articulated with clarity. Compromising on competency in the name of some other purpose—tokenism, diversity, payback, desperation—will not advance the cause of effective leadership. Similarly, issues of character must be confronted, not in hushed tones as an afterthought, but with the firm conviction that just as a leader requires certain technical knowledge and must possess the ability to adapt and communicate, communal heads and the enterprises they lead must be of impeccable moral quality. The same level of energy expended in vetting an individual's skill sets and eleemosynary predispositions must also characterize the consideration accorded his or her character. Even the illusion of impropriety must be addressed. Jewish organizational leaders must be individuals who take responsibility for their own behaviors, admit their mistakes, keep their word, and tell the truth even when doing so is risky and unpopular. They must be able to grow their organizations while remaining unscathed by the deleterious impact money can have upon leaders. The ubiquitous need for fiscal resources must, like any other business challenge, be dealt with without compromise to the integrity of either the leadership or the followership.

These are ongoing challenges. Competence and character are not things to be evaluated one time only. Rather, maintaining both requires a willingness to raise these issues at the highest level of communal discourse. They must be monitored consistently, and they must be incorporated as a regular part of leadership training programs. On many occasions, the organizations and institutions of American Jewry, anxious about their financial futures and about who will assume leadership roles and tempted to take the first available options, fail to think seriously about the efficacy of those "who exercise authority." Judaism's classical sources have much to teach about such issues. Their wisdom deserves a place not merely in the classrooms and sanctuaries but in the boardrooms of the American Jewish community as well.

NOTES

1. See, for example, Gary Yukl, *Leadership In Organizations* (Upper Saddle River, NJ: Prentice Hall, 2002), 175–204.

2. *Bava Batra* 8b. In discussing the importance of trustworthiness in leadership, the late esteemed leadership expert Peter Drucker once called Harry Truman "one of the most effective presidents of the last 100 years." Explained Drucker, Truman "didn't have an

ounce of charisma. Truman was as bland as a dead mackerel. Everybody who worked for him worshipped him because he was absolutely trustworthy. If Truman said no, it was no, and if he said yes, it was yes. And he didn't say no to one person and yes to the next one on the same issue." See Rich Karlgaard, "Peter Drucker on Leadership," *Forbes* 2004, http://www.forbes.com/2004/11/19cz_rk_1110drucker_print.html (accessed 8 Aug. 2005).

3. Exodus 18:21 (emphasis added).

4. Warren Bennis, *On Becoming a Leader* (New York: Basic Books, 2003), 23.

5. Moses Maimonides, *Mishneh Torah*, Book of Judges, Laws of Sanhedrin, 2:1.

6. Patrick Lencioni, *The Five Dysfunctions of a Team* (San Francisco: Jossey-Bass, 2002), 18.

7. A particularly striking example of this dynamic, drawn from contemporary Jewish life, is the 1999 merger that created the United Jewish Communities from three previously independent organizations. In their analysis of this historic event, Gerald Bubis and Steven Windmueller detail the missteps and misunderstandings that resulted when leadership prowess in one area (for-profit organizational management) was assumed to have automatic transferability in another (the organizational infrastructure of the American Jewish community). See their *From Predictability to Chaos?? How Jewish Leaders Reinvented Their National Communal System* (Baltimore: Center for Jewish Community Studies, 2005).

8. Warren G. Bennis and Robert J. Thomas, *Geeks and Geezers—How Era, Values, and Defining Moments Shape Leaders* (Boston: Harvard Business School Press, 2002), 91.

9. Moses Maimonides, *Mishneh Torah*, Book of Judges, Laws of Sanhedrin, 2:6.

10. Maimonides's insights are substantiated by the research of James M. Kouzes and Barry Z. Posner in *The Leadership Challenge* (San Francisco: Jossey-Bass, 1995), 209–41. Kouzes and Posner studied effective leaders and documented the importance of what they called "modeling the way." Their findings suggest that all those who wish to become successful leaders would do well to "Set the Example," and "DWYSYWD—Do What You Say You Will Do."

11. Deuteronomy Rabbah 2:19.

12. G. T. Fairhurst and R. A. Sarr, *The Art of Framing: Managing the Language of Leadership* (San Francisco: Jossey-Bass, 1996), xiv.

13. Frederic M. Jablin, "Communication," in *Encyclopedia of Leadership*, eds. George R. Goethals, Georgia J. Sorenson, and James MacGregor Burns (Thousand Oaks, CA: Sage Publications, 2004), 222.

14. Bennis, *Becoming a Leader,* xxiv. Studies of the American presidency also point to the importance of character in leadership. See Robert A. Wilson, ed., *Character Above All* (New York: Touchstone, 1995) and David Gergen, *Eyewitness to Power* (New York: Simon and Schuster, 2000).

15. Israel Isserlein, *Terumat ha-deshen, Pesakim u-ketavim*, 214.

16. In Hebrew, the word *elohim* can mean both gods and judges. The rabbis were often known to analogize the two. See, for example, Ruth Rabbah 1:1.

17. *Shulhan Arukh, Hoshen Mishpat*, 37.

18. Jerusalem Talmud, *Bikkurim* 3:3.

19. Moses Maimonides, *Mishneh Torah, Talmud Torah* 3:10.

20. Israel Bettan, *Studies in Jewish Preaching* (Cincinnati: Hebrew Union College Press, 1939), 287.

21. Yaakov Yosef, *Toldot Yaakov Yosef*, Lemberg Edition, 188a, cited in Samuel H. Dresner, *The Zaddik* (Northvale, NJ: Jason Aronson, Inc., 1994), 97.

22. Yaakov Yosef, *Toldot Yaakov Yosef*, 127c, cited in Dresner, *Zaddik*, 97.

23. Yaakov Yosef, *Zafnat Paneah*, Lemberg Edition, 16b, cited in Dresner, *Zaddik*, 102.

24. Kalonymus ben Kalonymus, *Even Bohan*, cited in Haim Hillel Ben-Sasson, "The Middle Ages," in *A History of the Jewish People*, ed. H. H. Ben-Sasson (Cambridge: Harvard University Press, 1976), 516.

25. For more on crown rabbis, see Simon Schwarzfuchs, *A Concise History of the Rabbinate* (Oxford: Blackwell, 1993), 135–36.

26. Michael Lerner, *Jewish Renewal* (New York: HarperCollins, 1994), 2–3.

27. Micah 3:9–11.

28. Exodus 18:21.

29. Moses Nahmanides, *Commentary* on Exodus 18:21.

30. Moses Maimonides, *Mishneh Torah*, Book of Judges, Laws of Sanhedrin, 2:7.

31. See Deuteronomy 16:19.

32. Salo Baron, *The Jewish Community*, Volume I (Philadelphia: The Jewish Publication Society of America, 1948), 98.

33. For additional information on taxation in medieval Jewish communities, see Dean Phillip Bell, *Sacred Communities: Jewish and Christian Identities in Fifteenth-Century Germany* (Boston and Leiden: Brill Academic Publishers, Inc., 2001); Jacob Katz, *Tradition and Crisis* (New York: Schocken Books, 1993); and Eric Zimmer, *Harmony and Discord: An Analysis of the Decline of Jewish Self-Government in 15th Century Central Europe* (New York: Yeshiva University Press, 1970).

34. The Jerusalem Talmud (*Sanhedrin* 2:6) alludes to the extra costs associated with communal prominence when one of the sages (Rabbi Hanina bar Sisi) was criticized for splitting his own wood, rather than hiring someone to help him. Concerned about the impact on his colleague's dignity and reputation, Rabbi Yohanan said to Hanina, "If you could not afford to engage help, you should not have accepted high office."

35. Rashi, Commentary on Exodus 18:21.

36. *Sefer Hasidim*, par. 1337; cited in Ivan G. Marcus, *Piety and Society: The Jewish Pietists of Medieval Germany* (Leiden: E. J. Brill, 1981), 91.

37. Leviticus 16:17. Also see Leviticus 8:14.

38. Ronald A. Heifetz and Marty Linsky, *Leadership on the Line* (Boston: Harvard Business School Press, 2002), 90.

39. There is some recent evidence to suggest that leadership experts from the corporate world are beginning to embrace similar views. See, for example, Chip R. Bell, "The Vulnerable Leader," *Leader to Leader* no. 38 (Fall 2005): 19–23.

40. I Kings 8:46, also II Chronicles 6:36.

41. Cited in Byron L. Sherwin, *Workers of Wonders* (Lanham, MD: Rowman & Littlefield Publishers, Inc., 2004), 112.

42. Leviticus 4:22–24.

43. *Horayot* 10b. Rabbi Johannan bases this interpretation on a wordplay of sorts. In the Torah the verse reads "*Asher nasi ye'hetah*—In case it is a chieftain who incurs guilt . . ." Instead of reading *asher* "In case," he reads *ashrei* "Happy."

44. Moses Maimonides, *Mishneh Torah*, Book of Knowledge, Ethical Ideas 2:6.

45. Cited in Menachem Elon, "On Power and Authority: The *Halakhic* Source of the

Traditional Community and Its Contemporary Implications," in *Kinship and Consent*, ed. Daniel J. Elazar (New Brunswick: Transaction Publishers, 1997), 317.

46. For a discussion of the importance of honesty in leading twenty-first-century corporations, see Herb Baum, "Transparent Leadership," *Leader to Leader* no. 37 (Summer 2005): 41–47.

47. For more on the differences between managers and leaders, see John P. Kotter, "What Leaders Really Do," and Abraham Zaleznik, "Managers and Leaders—Are They Different?" both in Harvard Business Review, *On Leadership* (Boston: Harvard Business School Publishing, 1990), 37–60; 61–88.

48. *Shabbat* 153a; *Avot* 2:15.

49. See, for example, the practices of Isaiah Horowitz's father and the hasidic master Levi Yitzhak of Berditchev, described in Byron L. Sherwin and Seymour J. Cohen, *How To Be A Jew* (Northvale, NJ: Jason Aronson Inc., 1992), 64.

50. Exodus 32:30.

51. Numbers 14:13–18.

52. Deuteronomy 34:10–12.

53. For more on the prophets as change agents, see Joseph Blenkinsopp, *Sage, Priest, Prophet: Religious and Intellectual Leadership in Ancient Israel* (Louisville, KY: Westminster John Knox Press, 1995), 144.

54. Isaiah 1:4–17; Amos 2:4–16.

55. Jeremiah 7:21–23.

56. *Sanhedrin* 89a.

57. Bennis, *Becoming a Leader,* xxi; 45–6; 105–32.

58. Jerusalem Talmud, *Sanhedrin* 3:8, 21c.

59. Exodus 23:2; *Sanhedrin* 2a.

60. *Sanhedrin* 38a; *Tanhuma, Pinhas* §10.

61. Abraham J. Heschel, *The Prophets* (New York: Perennial Classics, 2001), 22; 14 (emphasis included). An example of a prophetic message of consolation that follows a sharp critique appears in Isaiah 10:20–23.

62. On the imperative of doing so, see Heifetz and Linsky, *Leadership on the Line*, 101–22.

63. United Jewish Communities, *The National Jewish Population Survey 2000–01: Strength, Challenge and Diversity in the American Jewish Population* (New York: United Jewish Communities, 2003), 7.

Chapter Seven

The Behaviors of Effective Leaders

Having established the general precept that, in Judaism, successful leaders must be both competent and of unassailable character, many are still likely to be asking the question: Which behaviors are most likely to assure a leader's overall efficacy? After all, it is one thing to acknowledge that effective leaders are adaptable, possess good communicative abilities, and are resolute in refusing to accept bribes. It is quite another to delineate a list of behaviors that can actually help those with titled positions become better leaders.

Readers schooled in popular American business and political literature may be frustrated to learn that, from a Jewish perspective, as in the real world, no such list exists in a discrete and comprehensive form. Today, it is extremely popular, in a variety of media, to depict effective leadership as no more complicated than online shopping—simply select the desired behavior, "click" it into your personal "cart," proceed to checkout, and then get ready for a brilliant career as an effective leader. American Jews, routinely bombarded by trendy theories that try to reduce complex issues to simplistic formulations, can almost be forgiven for wanting effective Jewish leadership compacted into magic formulae.

As a practical matter, however, the expectation that a punch list of effective leadership behaviors will simply alight from these, or any other pages, in ready-to-use fashion, is naïve and ill conceived. The plethora of books from the general community, each purporting to contain *the* definitive listing of desirable behaviors, is the best proof that no such overarching taxonomy exists anywhere. Serious students recognize that isolating the behaviors of effective leaders is often highly subjective. In the case of Jewish leadership, this issue is further complicated by the fact that no body of traditional Jewish literature, not the Bible, the Talmud, or any of the later classical writings, contains a singular, definitive work dedicated exclusively to leadership. Instead, Jewish authorities wrote about many aspects of leadership in a diversity of works across the ages. Most of what has been written is highly specific and particular to a time period or set of circumstances; very little is generalized or systematic. For this reason, those who seek guidance and inspiration from the array of classical sources presented in this book and who wish to apply them in their work must actually study them, both alone and with others, plumbing their depths, contemplating their insights, extrapolating, and interpreting them over time, as serious Jews have always done. Even after doing so, however, attempts to develop a sweeping taxonomy of effective Jewish leadership behaviors will fall short of the ultimate goal. In the end, any such classification, including the one that follows, represents at best *a* listing, not *the* definitive Jewish word on the behaviors of effective leaders.

With that in mind, this chapter proposes a set of six behaviors that, with consistency, emerge throughout Jewish writings as characteristic of effective leaders. (There is nothing particularly sacred about the number six in this context. Indeed, some may wish that the concepts were enumerated differently. They should feel free, after appropriate study, to delineate their own listing.) The six behaviors are piety, tenacity, compassion, service to followers, humility, and consistency.

Clearly, these behaviors are not radically dissimilar from those thought to make for efficacious human beings generally. In part, this is because (as noted) the Torah understands the Jewish people to be *mamlekhet kohanim*—a kingdom of priests—that is, an entire nation of people capable of leading. Unlike some of the more fashionable categorizations of leadership behaviors found in the general literature, Jewish principles may strike some as remarkably commonplace and ordinary, rather than elitist and exceptional. In this regard, Judaism's approach is mirrored and validated by a handful of new research that draws very similar conclusions. Daniel Goleman, for example, whose research into emotional intelligence in the general population is well known, has recently observed that when it comes to effective leaders, those behaviors "that distinguish someone as a human being also distinguish him or her as a leader."[1] A related sentiment comes from one of the country's preeminent thinkers on leadership, Warren Bennis. In the introduction to his classic work, *On Becoming a Leader*, Bennis observed, ". . . the process of becoming a leader is much the same as the process of becoming an integrated human being . . . At bottom, becoming a leader is synonymous with becoming yourself."[2] Fourteen years later, in the introduction to the revised edition of the same book, Bennis concludes, "I am surer now than ever that the process of becoming a leader is the same process that makes a person a healthy, fully integrated human being."[3]

To the consternation of many, there is no simple formula or incantation that can be recited to acquire these six behaviors. Nor will merely incorporating them into daily life automatically make one a leader. Nonetheless, these behaviors are essential for anyone who wishes to don the mantle of authentic and effective Jewish leadership. There is a talmudic teaching that a person who is *obligated* to fulfill a commandment, and does, is greater than someone who just happens to perform the same act volitionally or by happenstance.[4] The equivalent may be said of leadership and the behaviors that follow. While all persons may share a theoretical duty to be pious, tenacious, compassionate, helpful, humble, and consistent, the urgency of doing so becomes most apparent in the case of those who occupy positions of leadership.

~

PIETY

Ideally, Jewish communal leaders (regardless of portfolio) must be pious individuals whose work is informed by a sense of both sacred mission and purpose. Piousness here is not the same as observance. In Judaism who a leader is and how a leader behaves matter more than policy pronouncements, titles, or other external measurements of effective leadership. When Jethro counseled Moses to select leaders who were God-fearing individuals, he understood that followers pay particularly close attention to how leaders conduct themselves, even on issues that seem unrelated to the performance of their work. There is a well-known hasidic tale told about Aryeh Leib Sarahs (1730–1791), disciple of the famed *maggid* (storyteller) of Mezhirech (Dov Baer, d. 1772) that underscores this point. When asked to expound on the nuances of law and biblical interpretations he learned from the great *maggid*, Aryeh Leib responded, "I did not go to the *maggid* to learn Torah from him, but to watch him tie his boot laces." This loyal follower understood that, many times, the seemingly insignificant actions of a leader provide followers with enormous insights and valuable lessons.

Today's communal leaders are rarely taught to consider the impact their personal behavior has upon constituents or the fact that followers pay attention to these matters at all. Even the best leadership training programs tend to avoid exploring the idea that a single individual can influence countless numbers of followers based only upon personal conduct. Judaism, however, insists that the way a leader behaves serves as a standard against which followers measure themselves and others. This is what the rabbis meant when they argued that the "body follows the head"[5] and that "whatever the leaders do, the masses do."[6] Similarly, the *Zohar*, the thirteenth-century classical work of Jewish mysticism, contends that followers not only *observe* their leaders' behaviors, they emulate them, either for good or for bad. "The acts of the leader are the acts of the nation. If the leader is just, the nation is just. If the leader is unjust, the nation too is unjust . . ."[7]

Recognizing this connection and certain that piety is not the exclusive province of the religious alone, the Torah stipulated expectations about godliness even for high-ranking "secular" leaders, namely the king:

> But it shall be when he sits on the throne of his kingdom he is to write himself a copy of this Instruction (*Torah*) in a document before the presence of Levitical priests. It is to remain beside him, he is to read out of it all the days of his life, in order that he may learn to have awe for YHWH his God, to be careful concerning all the words of this Instruction and these laws to observe them . . . [8]

Thus, even the monarch was expected to be pious. In the Torah's view, a pious king is a more effective king. By dint of having to follow divine law, for example, the sovereign was to be an empathic leader. He was proscribed from abusing his power or lording his position over his own subjects. A king bound by the same laws as his followers was in a much better position to relate to them, and they to him. A pious king is a more human king, willing to acknowledge mistakes, capable of transcending transgressions, and serving as both a model and an inspiration for followers.

Understandably, the idea of piety as a behavioral expectation for community leaders may leave many who currently hold titled positions feeling either intimidated or unprepared, or both. Alternately, it may serve to alienate those who say, "I'm willing to work on behalf of my temple, federation, JCC, or the like, but I'm not religious; I'm definitely not pious, and one thing has nothing to do with another." It is certainly the case that premodern metrics of piousness may need to be recrafted in a world in which even the word itself is off-putting to many.[9] Nonetheless, the tradition's contention that pious behavior is, indeed, a hallmark of effective leadership cannot be dismissed cavalierly. Truly successful Jewish leaders must stand for something greater than themselves or even their particular organization. Their work, whether as volunteers or professionals, must bespeak a palpable Jewish passion and commitment. Their values must be Jewish values, their mission a Jewish mission. This is not about being "religious" in some precisionist fashion. Even in earlier epochs, when a leader's fealty to *halakhah* was an expected precondition, piety was always about something more, something greater.[10] To behave piously, a Jewish leader must imbue his or her work with a sense of *kedushah*, of holiness. This is manifested not only in the obvious aspects of one's efforts—raising money for a Jewish cause or serving as an officer of a religious institution—but in the ways a leader comports him- or herself, both in public and in private; the manner in which he or she treats others, makes decisions, argues and disagrees, builds coalitions and countless other components of the leadership experience.[11]

However or whatever one chooses to observe then, a Jewish leader must reflect a sense of transcendence and elevated purpose in all of his or her efforts. Others may get lost in the bureaucratic morass that often characterizes Jewish organizational and congregational life. Leaders, however, must understand the broader context in which their work is done; they must remain fixed on a higher goal. A pious Jewish leader in the twenty-first century is not afraid to refocus followers, to remind them of the Ultimate in what they do, even when daily exigencies seem to predominate. Pious leaders keep both their work and their worth in perspective. They remain cognizant of their own strengths and limitations. They are committed to building a communal system in which human power—their own and others'—is circumscribed and shared. They are devoted to creating Jewish communities that are balanced in which all three *ketarim* have a treasured place at the table of communal deliberations.

Pious Jewish leaders seek to assure that their own organizations and communities reflect genuine Jewish values and precepts in all of their agendas. For today's Jews, this means that institutional leaders must address their own personal level of Jewish learning and literacy before they will be successful. They need to approach this task not with embarrassment or apology but with a profound understanding that learning is the key to piety.[12] Indeed, as the rabbis point out, "An unlearned person is incapable of truly being pious."[13] This is not because those who are uneducated are of inherently inferior character. Rather, it is because, as a practical matter, the head of a Jewish group who is incapable of identifying the very Jewish values and ethics he or she claims to stand for is perpetuating a myth. If the only thing motivating a Jewish leader is the desire to build a better organization, the message will quickly fall on deaf ears. In order for today's Jewish leaders to apply the values and teachings of Jewish tradition to the work they do in community, and thus provide their followers with an authentic and genuine sense of Jewish mission, they must be serious about Jewish learning, not just for others, but for themselves as well. When Jewish leaders personally commit to the enhancement of their own Jewish study, in whatever fashion and at whatever level is appropriate, they are modeling behavior and setting a standard for others. More importantly, they are in the truest sense behaving like Jewish leaders. The sages of the Talmud debated this question: Which is more important, learning or observing? Ultimately, they insisted that learning trumps everything else because "study leads to action."[14] A Jewish leader may invoke Jewish values as some vague and inchoate mantra. But unless that leader is knowledgeable, she or he will be unable to apply those lessons to the daily realities they and their followers must confront. Jewish leaders learn because learning and piety are interrelated. When a Jewish leader is a Jewish learner, then his or her pious deeds will influence countless others both "to learn" and "to do."

Above all else, pious Jewish leaders are driven by a genuine desire to do God's work. Sadly, fundamentalism of both the Jewish and non-Jewish variety has caused many Jewish communal leaders to shun this idea of divine service. Today, overt mention of God in the context of community leadership strikes many modern Jews as extremist. Some prefer to characterize their work in secular terms, deracinated from any sacred underpinnings. They refer to it as "community-building," "organizational development," or "Jewish continuity." Linking philanthropy, community relations, or education to Godliness rarely occurs to those who work on behalf of the Jewish community.

To the pious leader, however, doing God's work is not about certitude or excluding the views of others. It is not about religious fundamentalism. Doing God's work is the way pious leaders contextualize the processes of community leadership, not as a marketing ploy, but because they truly understand the holiness of what they do. They see a difference between expanding an organization and serving God, even if they both involve similar mechanics. Increasing membership, reaching campaign goals, and hiring a staff are the concerns of organizational bureaucrats. Building meaningful Jewish connections, providing for those in need, transmitting Torah, and raising the next generation of committed, passionate Jews are the challenges faced by pious leaders who see their work as an attempt to serve both God and the Jewish people.

In the context of this discussion, it is appropriate to mention that, in Judaism, piety is not the same as sanctimony. Indeed, it is safe to say that leaders who take pride in their piousness have missed the larger point. Leaders who do good work, who live righteously, who engage in ongoing learning, who treat others with dignity, and who imbue their efforts with a daily dose of the divine have no need to tell others how wonderful they are. Their deeds, not their words, are their best advocates. The all-too-familiar leader whose zeal quickly degenerates into self-righteousness and condescension makes a mockery of piousness.

Ironically, this principle is particularly relevant today as more and more Jewish leaders have begun to reevaluate their own levels of Jewish education and have dedicated themselves to serious study as a vital component of their leadership. While this is a most positive development, these individuals would do well to be on guard against the holier-than-thou attitudes that often seem to accompany such expanded learning. While Judaism revels in leaders who learn, it reviles those who laud their learning. One of the classical works of Jewish ethics, Moses Hayyim Luzzato's (1707–1747) *Mesillat Yesharim* (*The Path of the Upright*) addresses this very issue in words that ought to resonate with many who hold office in the contemporary American Jewish community.

> The possession of learning, for example, makes dangerously for pride and self-esteem, since it is an advantage that accrues wholly to the intellect, which is the highest faculty of the human being. Yet there is no one so learned who does not make mistakes, or who is not in need of learning from his equals, and at times even from his disciples. How, then, shall a man dare to boast of his learning? . . . A man of understanding, who has acquired more knowledge than the average person, has accomplished nothing more than what his nature impelled him to do, as it is the nature of the bird to fly, or of the ox to pull with all its strength. Hence, if a man is learned, he is indebted to natural gifts that he happens to possess. And any one gifted by nature with a mind like his would be just as learned . . . [15]

Similarly, while Judaism insists that pious behavior is the authentic standard against which all effective Jewish leaders are to be measured, classical sources go out of their way to caution against what is termed "foolish piety." In yet another example of the sages' realism and keen insight, the Talmud castigates those who are obsessed with piety to the point of stupidity.

> A man sees a child struggling in the river and says, "As soon as I remove my *tefillin* (phylacteries), I will save him." And even as he is removing them, the child's life gives out. Or he sees a woman drowning in the river and says, "It is improper [because of the rules of modesty] for me to look at her while I rescue her." Each of these is a foolish pietist.[16]

Though the cases cited are taken from a particular point in time and may strike contemporary readers as too quaint to be relevant, a literal read misses the larger point. As many have experienced, it is not at all uncommon in today's Jewish community to find those who are so consumed with a particular cause or issue that their ability to lead is mitigated. Single-minded enthusiasm, however noble in its origin, if left untempered can easily morph into the functional equivalent of "foolish piety." When followers are alienated, alignment and consensus become impossible, and a leader's efficacy is undercut. Thus, even as today's Jewish leaders aspire toward greater piety, the Talmud's words, along with the teachings of Luzzato, should serve as much needed counterbalances along the way.

TENACITY

Judaism has long taught what many have come to experience firsthand: only those leaders tenacious enough to withstand challenge and opposition over a protracted period can hope to be effective. Inherent in the depths of human nature, and particularly resonant in the soul of the Jewish people, is a basic resistance to being led. Even the desire for assurance and guidance cannot offset the natural antagonism manifested in the face of human authority. Because leaders lead change, and change means loss and disruption, anger directed against a leader is inevitable. To be successful, therefore, leaders must develop the skills and abilities to persevere, even in the face of extreme resistance.[17]

Such perseverance begins with a clearly articulated, overarching view of where a leader wishes to go and how he or she expects to get there. Absent that vision, the already difficult work of leadership will be impossible. But, the mere possession of a compelling vision alone is not enough. Unless that vision is communicated and explicated over time with sensitivity and resoluteness, the likelihood of actualization is limited at best. Calming people's fears, validating their worth, and overcoming objections all take considerable will on the part of the leader. Impatience with, or insensitivity to, the concerns of followers is a form of arrogance that will eventually derail chances for success. However convinced one may be of a plan's value, unless followers understand the vision, appreciate its significance, and fathom its impact upon them, their enthusiastic support will remain elusive.

There are no shortcuts to effective leadership. The traps and obstacles that conspire against a leader's efforts are ubiquitous. Hard won progress that is months or years in the making can easily be set back in a fraction of time. What seems like support one day turns to sabotage the next. Leaders are attacked; their mental, emotional, and even physical well-being may suffer. Under such circumstances, it is not surprising that many leaders become disheartened and lose sight of the ultimate goal, however noble and worthy. In this real world, where lofty visions meet objections, resistance, and competing viewpoints, a leader's resolve may be the difference between success and failure. As the Talmud teaches:

> If someone tells you, "I have labored but not found," do not believe him. If he says, "I have not labored, but I have found," do not believe him. But, if he says, "I have labored and I have found," then believe him.[18]

This link between a leader's efficacy and his or her tenacity appears in a number of other classical Jewish sources, as well. The great rabbinic sage Akiva was lauded for his legendary perseverance. Well past the age when others had departed the halls of the academy in pursuit of economic satisfaction, the man who would become the esteemed Rabbi Akiva first began the process of study at the then incredibly late age of forty. As the story goes,

Akiva learned the importance of tenacity as he observed phenomena in nature. The erosive impact of water on a stone assumed metaphorical status in his mind. Noticing that a steady stream of water had cut deep into a rock, he is said to have concluded: "Is my mind harder than this stone? I will go and study at least one section of Torah." In spite of the insurmountable odds and enormous sacrifices he and his wife had to make in pursuit of his goal, Akiva persevered for years, ultimately becoming one of rabbinic Judaism's greatest luminaries.[19]

Rabbi Akiva followed in the footsteps of many tenacious Jewish leaders, most prominent among them Moses. When Moses, whose entire career was a testament to perseverance, sought to name his successor, God instructed him as follows: "Single out Joshua son of Nun, a man in whom there is spirit . . ." (Numbers 27:18). The rabbis were struck by this curious phrase, "a man in whom there is spirit." Reflecting what they themselves knew to be the realities of leadership, they explained it to mean a person "who will have the capacity to stand up to the spirit of each and every one."[20] In other words, as the rabbis understood it, no leader is immune from criticism and attack. Efficacy increases only when one is able to withstand the personal and ideological assaults that come with the territory. Successful leaders must be able to hold their ground, even as they respond to the individual concerns of their followers.

The Bible recounts that shortly before his death, Moses "called Joshua and said to him in the sight of all Israel: 'Be strong and resolute, for it is you who shall go with this people unto the land . . .'" (Deuteronomy 31:7). In the Torah's view, this combination of strength and resoluteness is key to a leader's success. The rabbis commented on this verse by imagining a more detailed conversation between the two leaders, in which Moses then said to Joshua: "The people I am turning over to you are still kids of the goats, being very young. Do not be provoked by what they do, even as their Lord was not provoked by what they did . . ."[21] Once again, the rabbinic literature reveals its tremendous insight and realism. Leaders must be prepared for the inevitability of resistance. This is particularly true in the case of a new leader (and especially if, like Joshua, that new leader is succeeding a long-serving, highly respected individual). Part of tenacity then, is having the self-control to keep one's cool and not give in to anger. As this commentary intimates, doing so is far from easy. Indeed, on more than one occasion, even God Himself was tempted to become enraged at His people's resistance. Yet, as God overcame His instincts, communal leaders must learn to do the same.

Similar sentiments are reflected in stories the sages told about their own contemporaries. Hillel, for example, was esteemed by his colleagues for his enormous self-discipline. He never lost his temper, in part, because he never lost sight of his ultimate goal. In one particularly well-known tale, the rabbis describe how Hillel endured insult, derision, and public humiliation from an unscrupulous follower. Despite the enormous provocation, however, he remained calm and answered his attacker's questions with dignity and quiet confidence.[22]

Patience and the ability to control one's temper are thus invaluable tools for the tenacious individual who wishes to excel as a leader. Traditional Jewish sources express particular concern about anger because of its corrosive capacity to undo an otherwise accomplished individual. "When a man becomes angry—if he is a sage, his wisdom departs from him; if he is a prophet, his prophecy departs from him . . . When a man becomes angry, even if greatness has been decreed for him by Heaven, he is reduced from his greatness."[23] In the rabbinic calculus, anger is variously linked to arrogance, egomania, and contempt for others.[24] Perhaps most egregious of all for a Jewish leader, anger is analogized to idolatry because an enraged individual supplants God's agenda with his or her own. "When a man is angry, even the Divine Presence is deemed by him as of no account."[25]

Moses Maimonides also emphasized this link between anger and irreverence, particularly in the case of community leaders. In his introduction to the mishnaic tractate of *Avot*, known as *Shemonah Perakim*, Maimonides sought to explain God's punishment of Moses following the incident at Meribah (Numbers 20:1–13). In one of the Bible's most discussed events, God instructed Moses to provide the thirsting Israelites with water by "speaking" to a rock. In frustration and desperation, Moses struck the rock instead. As a result of his disobedience he was denied entrance into the Promised Land. In explaining God's actions, Maimonides argued that a leader who loses his or her temper and patience is guilty of blasphemous behaviors. Leaders, he argued, have a special responsibility to control their rage, precisely because they are public persons whose actions are carefully watched and emulated.

> God was strict with him because for a man like him to be angry before the whole congregation of Israel in a situation which did not call for anger was, relative to such a man, tantamount to blasphemy. For they all modeled their actions upon his and studied his every word in hopes thereby of finding fulfillment in this world and the next. How, then, could anger be seemly in him, when it is, as we have made clear, a bad mode of behavior and has only bad psychological effects? . . . Everything Moses said and did was scrutinized by them.[26]

Impatience and anger in the face of challenge result in a loss of self-discipline and control. An infuriated leader is no longer able to instill the trust and confidence necessary to function effectively. Even loyal followers begin to question a leader's ability in the face of what appears to be irrational behavior. As the medieval ethical text *Orhot Zaddikim* (The Ways of the Righteous) noted:

> Observe that most men, when they become angry and persist in their anger, do not pay attention to what they do in their great anger, and they do many things in their anger which they would not do otherwise. For anger deprives man of his reasoning, so that he becomes even angrier and enters into dispute and recrimination . . .[27]

Leading a Jewish organization today is rarely an easy experience. Challenges to a leader's authority are commonplace, second-guessing of decisions is a regular occurrence. It is easy to grow weary of such work, easy too to lose one's patience and even one's temper. The old joke about the first Prime Minister of Israel could just as easily be told about Jewish communal leaders in America, as well.

> When President Dwight Eisenhower met with Israeli Prime Minister David Ben-Gurion, the American president said at one point: "It is very hard to be the president of 170,000,000 people." Ben-Gurion responded: "It's harder to be the prime minister of 2,000,000 prime ministers."[28]

Inherent in this well-known quip is an important lesson. Because every member of the Jewish people is theoretically capable of leading (*mamlekhet kohanim*), those who do hold communal office are more than likely to encounter considerable differences of opinion. They must be patient and steadfast if they hope to succeed. No Jewish leader can simply superimpose his or her will upon those the Torah called "a stiff-necked people."[29] Nor will anger, rage, or righteous indignation be enough to overcome resistance and opposition. Real change will be effectuated not by invoking rank, credential, or the largesse of one's philanthropy but rather by patience, tenacity, and the determination to actualize an overarching and compelling vision.

As the father of modern Zionism, Theodor Herzl well understood this lesson of leadership. *Im tirzu, ein zo aggadah*—if you will it, it need not be a dream—he insisted to the naysayers and detractors of the Zionist movement. Herzl, the dreamer, understood that the mere possession of a dream was not enough. Strength, patience, fortitude, and a single-minded determination are vital to a leader's long-term success.

COMPASSION

Tenacity, however, must be matched by a willingness to show compassion for the concerns of others. In Judaism, sensitivity toward followers is not a sign of weakness; it is the essence of good leadership. In contrast to a more macho conception, Jewish sources maintain that realizing a difficult goal is not impeded by a leader's compassion; rather, such conduct goes a long way toward easing the pain of change and disruption often associated with bold and visionary leadership. When a leader takes the time to consider a plan's impact upon those most affected and understands the underlying emotional reasons for resistance and objection, the likelihood of long-term success increases. Jewish sources insist that steadfastness and compassion are *not* incongruous; they are, in fact, complementary behaviors for an effective leader.

The rabbinic literature makes precisely this point in its assessment of two of the Bible's most powerful leaders, Moses and David. In speculating about God's reasons for selecting both of these individuals, the rabbis determined that it was their inordinate compassion that ultimately persuaded God of their suitability for national leadership.

> "The Lord tests the righteous (Psalms 11:5)." How does He test him? By having him pasture sheep. He tested David through sheep and found him to be a good shepherd . . . God said: "He who knows how to look after sheep, bestowing upon each the care it deserves, shall come and tend my people . . ." Also Moses was tested by God through sheep . . . God said: "Because thou hast mercy in leading the flock of a mortal, thou wilt assuredly tend my flock Israel." [30]

While Moses is conventionally thought of as the lawgiver and commander and David as the deft conqueror, the rabbis identified compassion as the single most important factor in each man's leadership success. Though neither actually realized his ultimate dream—Moses failed to see the people enter the Promised Land, and David was denied permission to build God's Temple—the sages esteemed their leadership based not on tenacity, but rather, on sensitivity. In Judaism, a leader's enduring impact is measured by concern for followers more than mere persistence.

The rabbis relate another story about Moses that makes it clear that, in their view, his compassion actually enhanced his performance as a leader. During the battle with Amalek (Exodus 17:12), the Jewish people's archenemy, the Torah notes that Moses oversaw the action while seated upon a stone. Incredulous at the thought of him being so discomfited, the sages asked, "Did Moses have no cushion or bolster to sit on?" They concluded however, that it was Moses himself who chose to eschew any battlefield luxuries. "Of course, but Moses said, 'When Israel are deep in distress, I must be in it with them.'" [31] In the end, taught the sages, it was this level of empathy from their leader that inspired the Israelites to endure and ultimately to become victorious.

This marriage of tenacity and compassion as a prescription for successful

Jewish leadership is reflected in a recent chapter of Jewish history, as well. In 2005, as the Israeli government faced the daunting task of withdrawing from the Gaza Strip and relocating thousands of emotionally-charged residents, its military employed a strategy that embodied these classical Jewish teachings on effective leadership. Not surprisingly, in a situation in which Israel's army and police forces were shuttering synagogues and carrying Jews from their homes, resistance was palpable. A number of residents had, at the government's request, moved to Gaza decades before as part of a comprehensive settlement policy. Many believed the area to be part of a divine plan for the Land of Israel. Though by the time of its implementation, the evacuation was believed by most Israelis to be the only chance to preserve a majority Jewish population in the country, even supporters feared the prospect of Jews fighting Jews.

The actual disengagement, however, avoided any casualties and was accomplished in a matter of days, not the weeks or months originally anticipated. Key to its success was the decision by the Israeli Defense Forces to govern their actions according to a plan, known in Hebrew as *"nehishut v'regishut"*—literally "determination and sensitivity." With steeled will and tenacity, the military and police knew what had to be accomplished. They were not about to equivocate or lessen their resolve even in the face of personal attacks, moral indignation, and charges of Nazism. On the other hand, as a matter of policy, sympathetic unarmed soldiers allowed angry residents to vent red-hot emotions. Some even paused to pray with residents before completing their mission. *Nehishut v'regishut*—determination and sensitivity—a formula for effective leadership in the spirit of classical Jewish teachings.

The task of leadership, whether military or organizational, is to find the right balance between compassion and tenacity, sensitivity and determination. By definition, leaders must make difficult, sometimes heart-wrenching decisions that will engender controversy, challenge, and opposition. They cannot be dissuaded by the onslaught of resistance, however impassioned. At the same time, understanding on the part of those in power improves chances for the implementation and acceptance of even the most contentious policies and enables many a lofty dream to become reality.

SERVICE TO FOLLOWERS

In the 1970s a leadership theorist named Robert Greenleaf popularized an approach he called "servant leadership."

The servant-leader is servant first . . . it begins with the natural feeling that one wants to serve, to serve first. Then conscious choice brings one to aspire to lead. He or she is sharply different from the person who is leader first, perhaps because of the need to assuage an unusual power drive or to acquire material possessions. For such it will be a later choice to serve—after leadership is established . . .[32]

Long before Greenleaf, however, Judaism insisted that, to be effective as community leaders, individuals had to behave as servants of the people, not as rulers. In the words of a nineteenth-century hasidic teacher, "When a man enters a society . . . he may choose between serving or ruling it. He is advised to choose the former."[33] While many who hold titled positions in today's Jewish world may think of themselves as returning a favor, fulfilling an obligation, repaying a debt, or proffering a skill, Jewish sources conceptualize communal leadership as nothing less than service.

The Book of I Kings provides great insight into this issue and the nature of the relationship that ought to characterize leaders and followers. When the new king, Rehoboam, son of Solomon, sought advice from his father's former counselors on how to lead effectively, he was told: "If you will be a servant to those people today and serve them, and if you respond to them with kind words, they will be your servants always."[34] While the language is a bit antiquated for contemporary sensibilities, the point is clear; effective leadership involves a reciprocal relationship between leaders and followers. According to the rabbis, this verse is designed to teach that anyone "who is appointed over a community becomes the servant of the community." This principle, they argued, applies equally to both religious and political leaders.[35]

Authentic communal leaders do not superimpose their will on others, believing that they know what is best. In Judaism, leadership means subordinating one's personal agenda to that of the community's. "In the past," the rabbis reminded recent appointees to prominent posts, "you were subject to your own governance. But henceforth, you are in service to the community."[36]

Servant leadership is consistent with Judaism's teachings that leadership is not restricted to a certain few. Commenting on the verses found at the end of Deuteronomy (29:9–10): "You stand this day, all of you, before the Lord your God—your tribal heads, your elders and your officials, all the men of Israel, your children, your wives, even the stranger within your camp, from woodchopper to waterdrawer . . . ," the rabbis observed that in the presence of God, communal officers are no greater than anyone else; "all of you are equal before Me."[37] Thus, leadership is about peers serving peers, not elites ruling subordinates.

As a result, effective communal leaders must endeavor to serve the entire community, not merely selected special interests. "If God has granted you the privilege of being a leader in Israel," counseled the late-nineteenth-century hasidic work *Derekh Emunah U'maaseh Rav*, "Let every man be important in your eyes, and not inconsequential. For you cannot know who is worthy and who unworthy. Man often looks upon a fellowman as despicable and worthless, but God looks into the very heart."[38]

For some, the authority and power that often accompany high office militate against a sense of service and contribute instead to an attitude of self-righteousness and arrogance. Such individuals would do well to remember that leaders and followers are mutually interdependent. To this end, a story was told about the *rebbe* of Ger, who, after many years of serving his own *hasidim*, was appointed to head the Kotzker sect, as well.

> When in his sixtieth year after the death of the Kotzker, the Gerer accepted election as leader of the Kotzker hasidim, the Rabbi said: "I should ask myself: 'Why have I deserved to become the leader of thousands of good people?' I know that I am not more learned or more pious than others. The only reason why I accept the appointment is because so many good men and true have proclaimed me to be their leader . . ."[39]

In Judaism then, followers are as responsible for a leader's successful tenure as the leader himself or herself. In such a model, a leader succeeds not by aggrandizing power, but by serving others.

To be sure, those who prefer a more conventional approach to leadership have leveled no end of criticism at this notion of the leader-as-servant. Greenleaf's ideas, for example, have come under considerable attack from those who charge that serving is incongruous with strong leadership. Such criticism, however, is predicated upon a misunderstanding of what it means to serve. In Judaism, servant leadership is not weakened or diminished leadership. On the contrary, serving the community is tantamount to serving God. It helps to bridge the gap between the celestial and the terrestrial. This is what Rabbi Jeremiah meant in the previously cited text from the Jerusalem Talmud, "He who occupies himself with communal needs is as one who occupies himself with the study of Torah."[40]

Servant-leaders nurture and empower followers. They are not concerned about self-promotion, but rather about the growth and development of others. Servant-leaders seek to engender a sense of teamwork; they continually aspire to keep others motivated. They set a tone of mutual respect and interreliance. Leaders who serve are not concerned about ruling or getting their own way; they strive to do what is best for the entire enterprise. A leader who serves others is not afraid to be challenged or to challenge, to admit mistakes, or to hold others accountable. Most assuredly, serving is not ruling. From a Jewish perspective, it is far more effective.

HUMILITY

Of all the behaviors Judaism associates with effective leadership, none ranks higher than humility. For those raised on a conventional approach to leadership, the idea of a humble, great leader seems counterintuitive. The romantic model, particularly popular in cinematic representations of military or sports heroes, is one in which a single, forceful individual rallies the troops and on the strength of his (almost always, *his*) dynamic personality alone, others are inspired to fight the battle or win the game. Rarely, would "humble" be the adjective used to describe such an individual. The same is true in the business and political arenas. Humility is not normally associated with take-charge presidents or powerful chief executive officers. In fact, there seems to be a general understanding that with power comes arrogance, and that the stronger the leader, the greater the ego.

Perhaps it is the fact that so many seem to have embraced this view that explains why Jewish sources are so sharply opposed to it. Or perhaps the Torah's characterization of the Jews as the humblest of all nations (Deuteronomy 7:7) caused subsequent authorities to rank humility among a leader's most important behaviors. Perhaps still, the prophetic commandment to "walk humbly" with God (Micah 6:8) had particular resonance for those whom He authorized as leaders.[41] In any event, the halakhic (legal) and folkloristic literatures of Judaism are steadfast in their assertions that humility, not ego, is key to a leader's greatness.

As the tradition views it, arrogance is a form of idolatry in which the conceited individual places his or her own concerns above God's commands. Community leaders, therefore, are cautioned against imperiousness and pomposity.[42] Indeed those who aspire to serve the community are counseled to "love work and hate the holding of public office."[43] Individuals who lead gently and humbly in this world are guaranteed positions of leadership in the world-to-come.[44] As seen, communal officials are reminded to lead with humility throughout their tenure, lest past indiscretions become an embarrassing source of popular discourse.[45]

The ideal Jewish leader, then, is both humble and resolute. The Bible's most noted leaders, for example, from Abraham, who described himself as "but dust and ashes" (Genesis 18:27) to Joseph and Daniel who each declined the praises proffered upon them,[46] to Saul and David, first kings of Israel,[47] are all described as modest individuals. Indeed, every king of Israel was enjoined specifically to be humble. This, it may be recalled, was the reason that each was commanded to keep a copy of the Torah with him and to consult it regularly.

> When he is seated on his royal throne, he shall have a copy of this Teaching written for him on a scroll by the levitical priests. Let it remain with him and let him read in it all his life, so that he may learn to revere the Lord his God, to observe faithfully every word of this Teaching as well as these laws. *Thus he will not act haughtily toward his fellows* or deviate from the Instruction to the right or to the left to the end that he and his descendants may reign long in the midst of Israel (emphasis added).[48]

As noted previously, Maimonides expanded upon this text, by stipulating specific examples of humble behaviors expected from a monarch.

> Just as Scripture accords great honor to the king and bids all pay him honor, so it bids him cultivate a humble and lowly spirit . . . He must not exercise his authority in a supercilious manner . . . He should deal graciously and compassionately with the small and the great, conduct their affairs in their best interests, be wary of the honor of even the lowliest. When he addresses the public collectively, he shall use gentle language . . . At all times, his conduct should be marked by a spirit of great humility . . .[49]

Postbiblical leaders were also renowned for their humility, most notable among these, the talmudic sages. While the ancient rabbinical system was strongly hierarchical, and the rabbis were entitled to considerable respect and a great many privileges and exemptions, the most esteemed of them routinely waived the benefits to which they could legitimately lay claim. Great sages regularly overlooked their own status and position and eschewed the honor accorded them to benefit others.[50] Humility is also cited as the basis upon which the legal opinions associated with the disciples of the great teacher, Hillel, are given precedence over those of the students of his rival, Shammai.

> For three years there was a dispute between the house [students] of Shammai and the house [students] of Hillel, the former asserting, "The law is in agreement with our views" and the latter contending, "The law is in agreement with our views." Then a heavenly voice issued announcing, "Both [views] are the words of the living God, but the law is in agreement with the rulings of the house of Hillel." Since, however, both are the words of the living God, what was it that entitled the house of Hillel to have the law fixed in agreement with their rulings? Because they were kindly and humble, they studied their own rulings and those of the house of Shammai, and were even so humble as to mention the words of the house of Shammai before theirs . . . This teaches you that one who humbles himself, the Holy One, blessed be He, raises up, and one who exalts himself, the Holy One, blessed be He

humbles; from the one who seeks greatness, greatness flees, but the one who flees from greatness, greatness follows.[51]

The significance of this text cannot be overstated. In a world in which erudition was paramount, casuistry an art form, and argumentation its own reward, the fact that humility emerged as the most treasured of all behaviors is enormously important. While persuasiveness is certainly a potent weapon in the arsenal of effective leaders, it is less important than acknowledging the opinions of others and recognizing that no one has a monopoly on the truth.

Humility was also the ideal for the hasidic *zaddik* or *rebbe*. All *hasidim* were cautioned against arrogance, but because the *rebbe*'s job was to facilitate *devekut* (adherence) between his followers and God, he had no time to worry about his own ego needs. Any personal preoccupation would take him further away from the difficult work of serving others and God. The *zaddik*'s goal was the total "annihilation of the self" (*bittul ha-yesh*). As the leader, he was to be impervious to either compliments or criticisms and to maintain, instead, a sense of complete equanimity (*hishtavut*). In every aspect of his life, the hasidic leader was to behave without pretense or affectation. Despite the many perquisites of his office, the *zaddik* was to "keep far away from pride and adopt the quality of humility and lowliness."[52]

Of all Jewish leaders, ancient and modern, none embodied humility more than Moses. In the Torah's words, "Now, the man Moses is exceedingly humble, more than any human who is on the face of the earth."[53] At the core of Moses's humility was his unwillingness to take credit for any of the accomplishments that might otherwise have been attributed to him.[54] When tapped by God to lead the people, his first inclination was to demur, suggesting that others were better qualified (Exodus 3:11). His readiness to acclaim God and his fellow human beings allowed him to focus on the tasks-at-hand without self-aggrandizement or posturing. His humble nature permitted him to share power comfortably with his brother, Aaron, whose skill sets served to complement his own. Moses's humility enabled him to nurture and support up-and-coming leaders, from Eldad and Medad to Joshua (see chapter 5). So secure was he in his own mission and so unconcerned with trying to gratify his own ego that he welcomed the prospect of identifying and preparing successors who would carry on the important work that he had begun.

Not only are significant Jewish leaders renowned for their modesty, but even God, Himself, according to the midrashic tradition, is humble. The sages interpreted the unusual plural formulation found in the creation account, "Let *us* make man in *our* image after *our* likeness" (Genesis 1:26), to mean that God was so humble that He sought the counsel of the ministering angels before creating human beings.[55] Furthermore, as a sign of His humility, God chose to reveal Himself to Moses from a lowly bush rather than from some other, more auspicious, venue.[56]

In the aggregate then, God's humbleness, coupled with the modesty of Judaism's greatest leaders, serves to underscore a fundament of the tradition, namely that humility and strong leadership are perfectly compatible. If God's potency is not compromised by His humble nature, then surely human beings need not worry that humility will in any way weaken their efficacy as leaders. To substantiate this point, the rabbis analyzed a series of biblical verses and concluded that "Wherever you find [mentioned in the Scriptures] the power of the Holy One, blessed be He, you also find His humility mentioned."[57] A similar thing was said of Moses, whose status as the most humble of all biblical personages did not prevent him from also being known as the greatest of all prophets, the only human being ever to see God face-to-face.[58]

The Jewish idea that humility and effective leadership are not incongruous has gained expanded popularity in recent years, owing to what has come to be known as "Level 5 Leadership," based on the work of management consultant, Jim Collins, author of the book, *Good to Great: Why Some Companies Make the Leap . . . And Others Don't.*[59] The concept of Level 5 leadership emerged from Collins's five-year analysis of American companies in which he sought to answer the simple questions, "Can a good company become a great company and, if so, how?" In Collins's words, a Level 5 leader is

> . . . an individual who blends extreme personal humility with intense professional will. According to our five-year research study, executives who possess this paradoxical combination of traits are catalysts for the statistically rare event of transforming a good company into a great one.[60]

Unwittingly, no doubt, Collins proved what Judaism has taught for millennia: that personal humility, including shunning public adulation and a willingness to give credit to others, lies at the core of great leadership. Moreover, he found the opposite to be true as well. "In two-thirds of the comparison companies, we noted the presence of a gargantuan ego that contributed to the demise or continued mediocrity of the company."[61] Importantly, Collins is not the only researcher to have come to this conclusion. In their own study of effective leaders, drawn from two entirely different generations (the so-called "geeks and geezers"), Warren Bennis and Robert Thomas also found that humble leaders are often the most effective.[62]

Perhaps the fact that Judaism's insights have been corroborated by such sophisticated research will inspire those who hold titled positions in the Jewish community to reflect upon and even incorporate the tradition's teachings into their own personal leadership styles. To this end, Jewish authorities

taught that humility is acquired through practice. In this regard, two premodern texts provide useful and surprisingly pragmatic advice for today's communal heads. The first comes from an ethical will prepared by a medieval
commentator and mystic, Moses ben Nahman (Nahmanides, 1195–ca.1270),
for his son.

> Let your voice be low, and your head bowed; let your eyes be turned earthwards and
> your heart heavenwards. Gaze not in the face of him whom you address. Every man
> should seem in your eyes as one greater than yourself. If he is wise or wealthy, it is
> your duty to show him respect. If he is poor and you richer, or if you are wiser than
> he, think in your heart, that you are guiltier, he the more innocent. If he sin, it is
> from error; if you sin, it is with design![63]

Additional practical counsel for contemporary community leaders is found
in the writings of Moses Hayyim Luzzato. In order to facilitate humility, he
taught, communal officers must begin to train themselves in what he called
the "habit" of humility.

> The training consists in gradually habituating oneself to act humbly by always keep-
> ing in the background, and by dressing modestly; for a man's dress may be respect-
> able without ostentation . . . If a man would recall that after all his greatness he will
> return to dust and be food for worms, surely then would his pride be humbled, and
> his arrogance forgotten . . . Secondly, let him consider the vicissitudes of life. The
> rich man often becomes poor, the ruler subservient, and the man of eminence sinks
> into obscurity. Since a man is thus liable to find himself occupying a station in life
> that he now looks upon with contempt, how shall he be proud because of the good
> fortune which he can never be sure will last? . . . [T]he chief hindrance to humility
> is ignorance or little knowledge. You will observe that the more ignorant a man is,
> the more conceited he is . . . Associating with flatterers, or making use of their ser-
> vices, is another hindrance to humility. There are people who, when they want a
> favor, have recourse to flattery . . . Human character, after all, is fickle, weak, and
> easily tempted, especially in respect to those things toward which it is naturally
> drawn. When a man, therefore, listens, to a glowing account of himself, from one in
> whom he has confidence, it works like poison, and before long he is caught in the
> net of pride and is destroyed.[64]

While emphasizing that all leaders must learn and practice humility, Jewish sources make two additional points that should be considered seriously by
those who occupy prominent positions. The first is to guard against spurious
humility. Like the arrogant pietists described earlier, those who take pride in
their own humility are deceiving themselves as well as their followers. Such
individuals feign humbleness when, in fact, they crave attention and power.
Luzzato's eighteenth-century description of this phenomenon continues to
resonate. There is a certain kind of leader, he argued, who is not satisfied

having every one praise him for the superior traits which he thinks he possesses, but he wants them also to include in their praises that he is the most humble of men. He thus takes pride in his humility, and wishes to be honored because he pretends to flee from honor . . . He refuses all titles of greatness and declines promotion in rank, but in his heart he thinks, "There is no one in all the world as wise and as humble as I." Conceited people of this type, though they pretend mightily to be humble, cannot escape . . . Such a man has been compared to a house filled with straw. The house being full of holes, the straw keeps on creeping through them, so that after a while every one knows what is within the house. The humility of his behavior is soon known to be insincere, and his meekness nothing but pretense.[65]

A related point to be considered is that while humility is a venerated behavior, timidity is not. If humility is used as a cover for inactivity or indecision, then it is just as dangerous as arrogance. Leaders must be willing to take appropriate risks, to stand up for their beliefs, and to challenge followers when doing so is in order. They cannot allow a false sense of humility to paralyze initiative or to weaken resolve. Similarly, humility must not be used as an excuse for failing to serve the community. Self-deprecation is not humility; it is anathema to God as surely as any abuse of power. Moses, himself, was castigated for hiding behind the veneer of excessive humility, instead of recognizing his own capacities and stepping forward when called upon. After being instructed to tell both Pharaoh and the Israelites of God's plan to free the slaves, Moses resisted, claiming that he was unprepared for the task. "But Moses spoke up and said, 'What if they do not believe me and do not listen to me . . . ?'" God, however, was unwilling to accept such specious modesty. "The Lord said to him, 'What is that in your hand?'"[66] False protestations of humility when used to avoid leadership merit the divine wrath. God's response is nothing short of a rhetorical condemnation. "Use the capacities with which you have been endowed (that which is "in your hand")," God tells Moses. "Do not hide behind meekness. Timidity is unacceptable." A leader can, indeed must, be humble without being weak.

CONSISTENCY AND FAIRNESS

In Judaism, a leader's ability to behave with consistency and fairness is central to his or her long-term success. This is true whether the leader is a congregational rabbi or a head of state. Followers need to be convinced that leaders care about them and that the decisions they make, regardless of scope or impact, are neither arbitrary nor capricious.

Even God is obligated to maintain this standard, according to the Torah. When He does not, as for example, in the case of His indiscriminate plan to destroy Sodom and Gomorrah, He is called to account.

Abraham came forward and said, "Will You sweep away the innocent along with the guilty? What if there should be fifty innocent within the city; will You then wipe out the place and not forgive it for the sake of the innocent fifty who are in it? Far be it from You to do such a thing, to bring death upon the innocent as well as the guilty, so that innocent and guilty fare alike. Far be it from You! Shall not the Judge of all the earth deal justly?"[67]

Jewish legal codes adopted this principle for all community leaders, insisting that arbitrariness and favoritism are tantamount to abuses of power. The question is not whether one technically possesses the authority to make a random decision; the larger issue is whether doing so is in the best interests of both God and the people who are to be served. Inspired by Abraham's audacity, some Jewish authorities went so far as to suggest that followers have a duty to challenge a leader's policies when they lack consistency and fairness.[68]

Since, as demonstrated, Judaism analogizes officers of the community to judges on a court, impartiality for them is considered as essential as it is for jurists. While pressures on Jewish leaders to proffer preferential treatment are real, and in many cases, even understandable, capitulating to such force compromises a leader's ability to serve the needs of the entire community. To be sure, it is natural for congregational rabbis to favor their most loyal supporters and for agency board members to go out of their way to take care of special friends. So too, educators can be forgiven for preferring the company of devoted students while fund-raisers are always more likely to heed the interests of major philanthropists. Nonetheless, the job of an effective leader is to transcend these influences and to maintain a consistent standard of fairness and equitability.[69]

To many involved in the daily work of running the Jewish community, this concern about consistency and fairness in leadership may seem excessive. It is true, they concede, that when a national politico behaves capriciously, efficacy is compromised. But, they argue, it hardly seems apt to apply the same measure to the lay and professional heads of communal organizations. After all, many of these individuals operate in a system in which partiality is standard procedure. The fact is, of course, that such thinking is naïve. Indeed, when it comes to direct impact upon followers, a leader's biases are often more pronounced in smaller, voluntary settings than in larger, compulsory ones. Regardless of the size of the enterprise, however, a leader must be able to assure followers of a basic commitment to fair-mindedness. When congregants do not believe the rabbi cares for them as much as for the so-called "regulars," they are less likely to feel welcome or valued. When younger members, or those whose lifestyle choices seem at odds with prevailing organizational culture, believe that policy decisions favor others over them, there is a disincentive for continued participation. When people of modest economic means repeatedly get the message that their contribution to the community pales in comparison to those who "really matter," they are more likely to disassociate themselves from organized communal endeavors. Before automatically dismissing these concerns or blaming low levels of communal participation on the rank-and-file, Jewish leaders would do well to look deeply into their personal leadership styles and to evaluate their own performances against this standard of consistency and fairness.

A leader's obligation to avoid arbitrariness and to behave fairly, however, does not mean that everyone must be treated the same. An effective leader recognizes that each follower is distinct and that needs differ from one to another. The wisdom of *Proverbs* that children ought to be raised "in their own way" (22:6), meaning that parents and teachers should seek to develop the unique strengths of each child as an individual, has much to teach leaders about the way they nurture followers as well. The most successful leaders know how to vary their leadership styles in response to circumstances at hand. Divergent situations require different approaches.[70] One size can never fit all. Strongly directed leadership may work in extremis while a more participatory style may be most appropriate in the absence of crisis. On still other occasions, a leader will effectuate the greatest success by delegating responsibility to followers.[71] Effective leadership then, involves a unique combination of consistency and adaptability, fairness and flexibility.

In contemplating the foregoing taxonomy of effective leadership behaviors, contemporary Jewish leaders would do well to keep in mind that unless personal assets are deployed carefully and with restraint, even the greatest attributes can become weaknesses. The Jerusalem Talmud teaches that "The Torah may be likened to two paths, one of fire and one of snow. If one turns too close to the first, he will die in the fire; too close to the second, he will die in the snow. What should he do? He should walk in the middle."[72] Simply stated then, if even the Torah has the potential to be misused to excess, the six behaviors of effective leaders discussed in this chapter—piety, tenacity, compassion, service to followers, humility, and consistency/fairness— certainly do as well.

As a result, Jewish leaders must walk a path of centrism and moderation. In the real world of federations and agencies, community institutions and congregations, a virtue left untempered will easily become a vice. Thus, for example, where a pious leader is often the source of inspiration and vision, piety in excess is sanctimony and often does more harm than good. Similarly, tenacity and stick-to-itiveness lie at the core of successful leadership. But when blind persistence and inflexibility militate against a willingness to consider objective realities, a leader's efficacy is destroyed. The same may be said of compassion and caring, both of which are likely to enhance the capacity and loyalty of followers. If, however, a leader's kindness attenuates his or her ability to demand excellence or challenge the established order, such behavior will likely undermine the growth of the enterprise. So too for the other behaviors of effective leadership; when serving followers becomes justification for passivity, or humility an excuse for indecision, or consistency a reason for tolerating incompetence, laudable behavior turns dastardly.

The medieval authority, Moses Maimonides, strongly influenced by Aristotle, recognized the potential for positive characteristics to be distorted by surfeit. To this end, he counseled all people to embrace the doctrine of the Golden Mean. In the section of the *Mishneh Torah* entitled "Laws of Ethical Conduct," he advised the following:

> Every human being is characterized by numerous moral dispositions which differ from each other and are exceedingly divergent . . . Between any moral disposition and its extreme opposite, there are intermediate dispositions more or less removed from each other . . . To cultivate either extreme in any class of dispositions is not the right course nor is it proper for any person to follow or learn it. If a man finds that his nature tends or is disposed to one of these extremes, or if one has acquired and become habituated to it, he should turn back and improve, so as to walk in the way of good people, which is the right way. The right way is the mean in each group of dispositions common to humanity: namely that disposition which is equally distant from the two extremes in its class, not being nearer to the one than to the other. Hence, our ancient sages exhorted us that a person should always evaluate his dispositions and so adjust them that they shall be at the mean between the extremes . . .[73]

To the extent that such instruction has application for all people, it surely merits special consideration by leaders of the community. In pursuit of long-term effectiveness, a leader's reasonableness and centrism will almost always prevail over extremism, even in the case of otherwise commendable behaviors.

These, then, represent six behaviors of effective Jewish leaders, extrapolated from centuries of Judaism's teachings and communal experiences. Those who hold leadership posts in today's Jewish world will have to decide how many of the six to incorporate into their own personal leadership styles and in what ways. Every one of these behaviors must be learned; no one is born with any of them. Acquiring them is a continuous process and will require a combination of study, self-awareness, and ongoing practice.

NOTES

1. Daniel Goleman, "The Emotional Intelligence of Leaders," in *On Mission and Leadership*, ed. Frances Hesselbein and Rob Johnston (San Francisco: Jossey-Bass, 2002), 30. Also see Daniel Goleman, "What Makes A Leader?" Reprint, *Harvard Business Review* (November–December 1998): 93–102.

2. Warren Bennis, *On Becoming a Leader* (New York: Basic Books, 2003), xxviii–xxxiii.

3. Bennis, *Becoming a Leader,* xxiv.

4. *Kiddushin* 31a.

5. *Eruvin* 41a.

6. Deuteronomy Rabbah 2:19.

7. *Zohar* ii (Exodus, *Beshalah*) 47a.

8. Deuteronomy 17:18–19.

9. A classic premodern definition of piety is found in Moses Hayyim Luzzato's *The Path of the Upright (Mesillat Yesharim)*. There, Luzatto (1707–1747) identifies "all the elements of perfect piety." These include: "fearing God, walking in His ways, loving Him, acting sincerely, and keeping all the commandments" (Author's Preface). Despite its eighteenth-century date, Luzzato's work clearly reflects medieval Jewish sensibilities.

10. In Hebrew the term is *lifnim mi-shurat ha-din*—going beyond the letter of the law. The Talmud and later authorities encourage scrupulous individuals to behave at a standard beyond that which is required by strict interpretation of the law. For a thorough list of relevant sources and additional explanations, see Menachem Elon, *Jewish Law: History, Sources, Principles*, Volume I (Philadelphia: The Jewish Publication Society, 1994), 155–67.

11. On the matter of treating others, the Talmud recounts the story of the pious sage Rabbi Zakkai, who was once asked to explain his long life. Zakkai speculated that, among other things, his longevity was attributable to the fact that he had so much basic respect for other people he would never even jokingly call someone by a nickname, even if that nickname was not derogatory (*Megillah* 27b). The point is that, in Judaism, how one treats others is no less an indicator of personal piety than how fervently one prays or how scrupulously one observes dietary laws.

12. See, for example, *Avodah Zarah* 20b. Also see Maimonides on the linkage between knowledge of God and the love of God in the *Mishneh Torah*, Book of Knowledge, Fundamentals of the Torah 2:2, and Laws of Repentance 10:6.

13. *Avot* 2:5.

14. *Kiddushin* 40b.

15. Moses Hayyim Luzzato, *Mesillat Yesharim*, chapter 22.

16. *Sotah* 21b.

17. For an expanded discussion of the linkages between change and resistance, see Ronald A. Heifetz and Marty Linsky, *Leadership on the Line* (Boston: Harvard Business School Press, 2002), 9–48; David A. Nadler, *Champions of Change: How CEOs and Their Companies Are Mastering the Skills of Radical Change* (San Francisco: Jossey-Bass, 1997); and David A. Nadler, Robert B. Shaw, and A. Elise Walton, *Discontinuous Change: Leading Organizational Transformation* (San Francisco: Jossey-Bass, 1995).

18. *Megillah* 6b.

19. *Avot de Rabbi Natan* 6.

20. *Sifre Zuta, Pinhas*, §16.

21. *Sifre* Deuteronomy, §305.

22. *Shabbat* 30b–31a.

23. *Pesachim* 66b.

24. Byron L. Sherwin and Seymour J. Cohen, *How To Be A Jew* (Northvale, NJ: Jason Aronson Inc., 1992), 84–85.

25. *Nedarim* 22b.

26. Moses Maimonides, *Shemonah Perakim*, "The Cures of the Illnesses of the Soul."

27. *Orhot Zaddikim*, "The Gate of Anger."

28. Joseph Telushkin, *Jewish Humor: What the Best Jewish Jokes Say About the Jews* (New York: William Morrow and Company, Inc., 1992), 82–83.

29. Exodus 32:9.

30. Exodus Rabbah 2:2.

31. *Taanit* 11a.

32. Robert K. Greenleaf, *Servant Leadership: A Journey into the Nature of Legitimate Power and Greatness* (New York: Paulist Press, 1977), 13. Also see Greenleaf Center for Servant-Leadership, "What is Servant-Leadership?" www.greenleaf.org/leadership/servant-leadership/What-is-Servant-Leadership.html (accessed 29 Aug. 2005).

33. M. Walden, *Ohel Isaac*, 3, cited in Louis I. Newman, *Hasidic Anthology* (New York: Schocken Books, 1963), 216.

34. I Kings 12:7.

35. *Yalkut* I Kings §197; *Horayot* 10a–b.

36. *Sifre* Deuteronomy, §16. Also see Exodus Rabbah 27:9 and *Shabbat* 54b.

37. *Tanhuma, Nitzavim* 2.

38. J. S. Cohen, *Derekh Emunah U-Maaseh Rav*, 9–10, cited in Newman, 217.

39. Abraham Alter, *Meir Einei ha-Golah* 2:29–30, cited in Newman, 218.

40. Jerusalem Talmud, *Berakhot* V, I, 8a.

41. Other prophets also warned those in power not to let their egos get out of control. In Jeremiah's words, "Let not the wise man glory in his wisdom, neither let the mighty man glory in his might, let not the rich man glory in his riches" (Jeremiah 9:22).

42. *Pesachim* 113b. Also Exodus Rabbah 27:9.

43. *Avot* 1:10.

44. *Sanhedrin* 92a.

45. *Yoma* 22b.

46. See Rashi and Elijah Mizrahi on Genesis 41:16 (Joseph) and Daniel 2:30.

47. See I Samuel 10:22 (Saul) and II Samuel 6:22 (David). Also see *Tosefta Berakhot* 4:18 for more on Saul's humility and Numbers Rabbah 4:20 for additional insights into the humility of King David.

48. Deuteronomy 17:18–20.

49. Moses Maimonides, *Mishneh Torah*, Laws of Kings, 2:6.

50. *Sotah* 40a; Ecclesiastes Rabbah 1:7, # 9.

51. *Eruvin* 13b.

52. See sources cited in Norman Lamm, *The Religious Thought of Hasidism* (New York: Yeshiva University Press, 1999), 441–52; Louis Jacobs, *Jewish Values* (Hartford: Hartmore House, Inc., 1960), 113–15; and Samuel H. Dresner, *The Zaddik* (Northvale, NJ: Jason Aronson, Inc., 1994), 142–47.

53. Numbers 12:3.

54. *Shabbat* 89a. Indeed, Nahmanides (*Commentary* on Numbers 20:8) explains that the reason Moses's transgression at the waters of Meribah (Numbers 20: 1–13) was adjudged especially egregious is that his actions led people to believe that he, not God, was responsible for providing the life-sustaining water; a clear departure from his usual behavior.

55. Genesis Rabbah 8:8.

56. Exodus Rabbah 2:5; *Sotah* 5a.

57. *Megillah* 31a.

58. Deuteronomy 34:10.

59. Other experts are also coming to appreciate the significance of humility in effective leadership. Without mentioning Judaism per se, MIT lecturer and acclaimed author, Peter M. Senge recently wrote: "We all have blind spots . . . But it is also within the human possibility to recognize our prejudices and discover our blind spots . . . It is why cultures around the world that have endured for hundreds and thousands of years invariably come to value humility as an attribute of real leadership. Without humility we cannot discover the biases in our own thinking . . ." See Peter M. Senge, "Missing the Boat on Leadership," *Leader to Leader* no. 38 (Fall 2005): 30.

60. Jim Collins, "Level 5 Leadership: The Triumph of Humility and Fierce Resolve," Reprint, *Harvard Business Review* (January 2001), 68.

61. Collins, "Level 5 Leadership," 72. The results of his findings are more fully explored in Jim Collins, *Good to Great: Why Some Companies Make the Leap . . . And Others Don't* (New York: HarperBusiness, 2001).

62. Warren G. Bennis and Robert J. Thomas, *Geeks and Geezers—How Era, Values, and Defining Moments Shape Leaders* (Boston: Harvard Business School Press, 2002), 83.

63. Cited in Jacobs, *Jewish Values*, 112.

64. Moses Hayyim Luzzato, *Mesillat Yesharim*, chapter 23.

65. Luzzato, chapter 11.

66. Exodus 4:2.

67. Genesis 18:23–25.

68. See, for example, Moses Maimonides, *Mishneh Torah*, Laws of Robbery and Lost Property, 5:14, and Responsum of *Ribash ha-Hadashot* #9.

69. Responsum of Rabbi Moses Isserles, 108.

70. See Robert Tannenbaum and Warren H. Schmidt, "How to Choose a Leadership Pattern," Reprint, *Harvard Business Review* (May–June 1973): 3–12.

71. Contemporary Jewish communal leaders looking for an authentically Jewish model for such an approach need look no further than Moses, himself. Committed as he was to leading fairly and equitably, with a demonstrated track record of challenging leaders (human and divine) when they behaved indiscriminately, Moses understood the imperative of adjusting his leadership to the particular needs of his followers and the exigencies of the day. Nurturing and ennobling under many circumstances, he demonstrated equal facility for issuing split-second decisions and unambiguous instructions when necessary. He was reticent and restrained on some occasions and remarkably bold on others. For more on this aspect of Moses's behavior, see my *Models and Meanings in the History of Jewish Leadership*, 11–12. Additional information on Moses as an effective leader is found in

Aaron Wildavsky, *The Nursing Father* (Tuscaloosa: The University of Alabama Press, 1984); and Ari Z. Zivotofsky, "The Leadership Qualities of Moses," *Judaism* (Summer 1994): 258–69.

72. Jerusalem Talmud, *Hagigah* 2:1, 77a.

73. Moses Maimonides, *Mishneh Torah*, Laws of Ethical Conduct, 1:1–4. Maimonides does make exceptions to the rule of the Golden Mean for pride and anger. See Laws of Ethical Conduct, 2:3.

Chapter Eight

Jewish Leadership for the Twenty-first Century

The story is told about Boris Yeltsin who, shortly after becoming Russia's president, held his first American-style press conference. "Mr. President," he was asked, "How is it going?" "In a word," he said, "good! In two words, not good."

The twenty-first-century American Jewish community could most certainly be described in similar fashion. On the one hand, there is much that can be considered good news. Rates of anti-Semitism in the United States are generally quite low. Rarely is being Jewish, even actively so, considered an impediment any longer in business, college admissions, politics, club membership, or home buying. The widespread acceptance of Jews in America has led to a reawakening in Jewish arts, culture, and publishing, unlike anything ever seen in this country. From books and magazines to film festivals, music, theater, dance, and fine arts, a diverse and talented group of Jewish artists is helping to redefine Jewish creativity and identity.

Today's Jewish world has witnessed an explosion in all forms of Jewish learning as well. From early childhood programs to day schools, from overnight camps to universities, quality Jewish educational opportunities abound across America. Teenagers and collegians have more opportunities to visit and study in Israel than ever before, and a variety of adult Jewish learning programs have sprung up nationwide in synagogues, Jewish Community Centers (JCCs), and private living rooms.

Congregations are reinventing themselves, as once moribund institutions are being brought back to life in what has become known across the country as the synagogue transformation movement. From the right to the left, the East Coast to the West, growing numbers of American synagogues are becoming spiritual centers, attracting not only *more* members but members with a deep sense of ownership and responsibility for the future of their congregations and for the quality of Jewish life within and beyond their doors.

On the other hand, however, there are a number of indicators that seem to point to the possibility of a precipitous decline in the quality of American Judaism. While in the previous century most of Jewish life was played out against the backdrop of organizations and communal institutions, in this century increased numbers of Jews are choosing to simply ignore or bypass the organized communal infrastructure. Traditional assumptions about what it means to be Jewish in America are being challenged and, in many cases, discarded. Where once Jews married other Jews, joined a synagogue, played ball at a Jewish center, gave their kids a Jewish education, affiliated with Jewish groups whose missions they supported, gave to Jewish charity, and had deep, personal attachments to the State of Israel, those things are happening less and less in this generation. In a free and open society, where Jews can go anywhere, do anything, and marry anyone, old ideas of what it means to be a "good" Jew are no longer compelling to many. Not only have intermarriage rates skyrocketed since the 1980s, which have had demonstrably deleterious effects upon the Jewish educational levels of the children of those marriages, but even among endogamous couples, traditional indicators of connections with the organized Jewish community are way down from previous generations.

Mirroring trends that reach across America, today's Jews are far more comfortable with episodic and intermittent linkages than with traditional forms of protracted affiliations, such as memberships, dues, and deep-seated organizational loyalties.[1] Today, Judaism has become a leisure-time activity; one of the many things American Jews do *if* they have the time and are so inclined. And even then, only on occasions that suit their needs, temperaments, and value systems. They do so without the slightest suggestion that such picking and choosing is bad or unacceptable. The days of "doing Jewish" out of guilt or some antiquated sense of group loyalty are long gone. Many of today's Jews see no reason to connect formally with the Jewish community. They don't believe they need institutions or organizations to be Jewish. As a result, there can no longer be any presumption that Jews will automatically send their kids to a Jewish school, join a Jewish Community Center or a congregation, give *tzedakkah*, or practice Judaism in any way, shape, or form. And if they do so once, there is no assurance that they will continue those patterns over the long term. American Jews, like their compatriots of other backgrounds, enjoy a world in which people download only the music they want to hear, record only the television shows they wish to watch, and read personalized newspapers containing articles selected just for them. In this on-demand world, they are hard-pressed to tolerate, even for a moment, anything that does not immediately satisfy their needs.

Against this broad continuum of Jewish life, ranging simultaneously (in the words of historian Jonathan Sarna) from assimilation to revitalization, the challenges confronting American Jewry have never been more daunting, and the future never more uncertain.[2] Rarely has the need for bold and visionary leadership ever been greater. And yet, the evidence is overwhelming: twentieth-century communal leadership models no longer resonate with many twenty-first-century American Jews. Today's generation seeks a different kind of leadership: one that is far more egalitarian and less hierarchical, one that is committed to the diversity of American Jewish interests rather than to a single demographic, and one that can be trusted to understand both the Jewish past and the Jewish future.

Ironic as it sounds, what many contemporary American Jews are searching for presupposes a return to the classical conceptions of leadership discussed throughout this book. These precepts are not relics from a bygone era, but rather, foundations upon which dynamic communal systems have been and can continue to be built. If allowed to do so, they will restore authenticity and effectiveness to American Jewish leadership and, by extension, will forge the next link in the ongoing chain of Jewish communal development.

In light of the realities of the current era then, there are four overarching principles drawn from the sources presented in this work, which ought to define American Jewish leadership in the twenty-first century.

BEHAVIOR NOT POSITION

Judaism's insistence that the essence of leadership is behavior, not position, is critically important in attracting and reenergizing a loyal followership in the twenty-first century. Equating leadership with title may have been quite understandable in prior epochs (and may still persist as a matter of convention), but, in truth, the mindset and value system of today's generation is far better suited to the traditional conception. By acknowledging that leadership and authority are not the same, that effective Jewish leaders may just as easily come from the ranks of the untitled—from those who have eschewed or been overlooked by the organizational infrastructure—the Jewish world can benefit immeasurably. Separating leadership and position in the true spirit of the Hebrew word *manhigut* (from the root meaning behavior) expands the possibilities for creativity in this new era and is consistent with highly successful models of earlier centuries.

Indeed, throughout Jewish history many of the most impressive cases of authentic leadership have come not from those who hold office but from those who have challenged the established order. Reflecting upon the American Jewish experience, for example, Professor Jonathan Sarna made the point that over the past 350 years, the inspiration, motivation, and direction for many of the major innovations and initiatives in American Jewish life came from women and men who exercised leadership *without* authority, not from those who held titled positions. This is true in the history of Jewish education, Jewish publishing, social services, early American Zionism, the Soviet Jewry movement, and to a large extent feminism and Jewish Renewal as well. In Sarna's words, "The most creative ideas for revitalizing Jewish life flow from the bottom up, rather than from the top down, and from outsiders rather than insiders."[3]

The ability to influence the Jewish future, therefore, need not be limited to the major philanthropists, rabbis, or executives of the American Jewish establishment. Nor is it restricted only to those who pay homage (or dues) to the organizational infrastructure. As new forms of thoughtful Jewish expression, from e-zines to cutting-edge philanthropy, are today making clear, leadership is, indeed, a behavior, not a position. It comes not only from those who hold a title but from those with the courage to step forward, to perceive a challenge or crisis, to articulate a vision, and to build a coalition of others who will embrace and follow that vision.

When the Israelites stood paralyzed at the Sea of Reeds, taught the rabbis, fearful of the pursuing Egyptians and too afraid to step into the water themselves, it was one man, Nahshon, son of Amminadab, who was bold enough to walk into the sea all the way up to his neck.[4] Only at that point, according to the sages, did the waters split, allowing the rest of the people to follow. Nahshon, son of Amminadab—not exactly president of the local federation or chairman of the temple brotherhood or even a name that most Jews could identify. In Judaism, great leadership has nothing to do with title or celebrity. Since leadership is a behavior, not a post, successful leadership is not limited to a certain few—to those with money, to those who look a certain way, or to those with prestigious credentials.

This does not mean, of course, that those who hold titled positions in the Jewish community (many of whom have worked long and hard to get there) are automatically disqualified from leadership. As the Talmud teaches, "Jephthah in his generation is to be considered as Samuel was in his generation." It does mean, however, that those currently in office must be particularly sensitive to the differences between leadership and authority; they must strive always to *behave* as leaders. Particularly because those with titled positions are often looked upon *as* leaders, regardless of their behavior, such individuals bear a special responsibility to earn the crown of leadership based upon their actions, not their office.

LEADERSHIP: THE PROVINCE OF
THE MANY, NOT THE FEW

Judaism's embrace of the idea that all Israel is *mamlekhet kohanim* (a nation in which all are theoretically capable of donning the mantle of leadership) has enormous resonance for a generation that has grown increasingly suspicious of iconic or lone-wolf leaders. In rejecting the notion that a single "great" leader will magically appear to unilaterally take charge and "fix" all that has gone wrong, classical teachings affirm what many in this generation have come to understand, namely that effective leadership is not the unique province of a select group of individuals endowed with a predetermined set of innate talents or attributes. Rather, leadership comes in a variety of forms.

Judaism's rejection of the conventional bifurcations between leaders and followers underscores the value of reciprocity and the importance of great followers to the success of any enterprise. Like the letters of the divine name, taught a hasidic master, leaders and followers are linked together in an inextricable bond. The expectations and conduct of followers are as determinative of a leader's performance as a leader's actions are potent and pivotal influences upon followers. "As the garden, so the gardener," teaches a *midrash*.[5] Judaism insists that followers give to their leaders at least as much as they receive; they are not powerless pawns. Followers, according to classical sources, are full partners with God in authorizing and legitimating the powers of their leaders.

Such an attitude strengthens leadership at every level of an organization. It opens doors for those who are young, creative, and energized while discouraging the tendency to place all the blame (or credit) upon a single individual or elite group. Judaism's recognition that an appeal for strong leaders is in fact a simultaneous call for strong followers, speaks directly to the sensibilities of many twenty-first-century American Jews. It charges them to keep in mind that, important as it is to have powerful leaders, followers have an enormous role to play, as well. Those who recognize the potency of their role and position, as followers, can never criticize institutional leaders without at least considering their share of responsibility. Further, they are duty bound to step forward when the situation demands it and not rest comfortably on the sidelines. Because leaders and followers are so closely linked, followers have both a right and an obligation to demand excellence from their leaders and to seek alternative actions when necessary. They are obligated to decry the excessive reliance on single "messianic" leaders that often accompanies times of radical change.

Happily, a new generation of Jews, serious about their Judaism, even as they disdain elements of the communal bureaucracy, has begun to do just that. They are working to forge creative responses to the current challenges facing American Jewry, despite their lack of official institutional status. These contemporary Jews, who choose not to believe that only certain types can lead, are pioneering new publications, social service initiatives, cultural and artistic expressions, worship and study opportunities, and volunteer giving projects across the country. Intuitively, they embrace the notion that there is no one single brand of leader, that in Judaism, leadership belongs to the many, not to the select few. They understand that in the twenty-first century, as in centuries past, leaders and followers in the Jewish world are equally vital partners in a dynamic relationship.

COMPETENCE AND CHARACTER

Twenty-first-century American Jews may be fed up with the institutional nature of American Jewish life, but many retain a deep spiritual yearning and a desire to incorporate certain aspects of Judaism into their lives. They may have little interest in what they consider to be organizational trifles and balderdash, but they have not severed all of their relationships with Jews, Judaism, and God. Their willingness to be part of Jewish life, albeit on their own highly personalized terms, suggests the urgency of restoring the premodern leadership ideal to the contemporary Jewish community.

Today's Jews are looking to their leaders for the combination of competence and character that has always been the standard (if not the reality) for Jewish communal leaders. The twentieth-century variant of American Jewish leader-cum-fund-raiser whose power derives solely from possessing or having access to wealth and connections, whose personal leadership style frequently conveys a sense of entitlement, and whose level of Jewish literacy is often little more than elementary no longer rings true for an entire generation of contemporary Jews.

Increasingly hardened and cynical about leaders as a result of the steady stream of business, political, and religious crises in America, today's Jews hope, if not expect, that, at a minimum, their own community will be headed by individuals who are (in the Torah's words) both capable and trustworthy. Followers want authenticity and integrity from their leaders. This means that leaders must stand for something beyond their own self-aggrandizement. It means they must be honest with themselves and with others and possess an unimpeachable personal moral code. For Jewish leaders, it also means a commitment to Jewish learning, for themselves, as well as for others. It means women and men who view their leadership not as a power trip or an opportunity to advance their own agenda but as sacred service to God and the people-at-large.

Beyond character, however, twenty-first-century Jewish communal leaders must be every bit as competent as those envisioned by traditional teachings. There is no reason why they shouldn't match, if not exceed, the levels of excellence associated with the best leaders in the general community. The sociological, demographic, spiritual, and educational challenges facing American Jewry today are overwhelming. They will not be addressed by organizational bureaucrats who merely perpetuate business as usual because they are unwilling to take risks or experiment. Only those organizations and institutions with "response-able" leaders, that is, leaders who are *able to respond* to the rapidly evolving needs of American Jews, will succeed in the long term. Individuals who are capable of *addressing, not merely finessing*, the great challenges of this era will alone earn the ongoing respect of an ever-changing Jewish polity. Bold, visionary leadership, not incremental, risk-averse management will compel the attention of today's Jews. Otherwise, as every recent demographic and attitudinal survey has shown, they will simply walk away.

A PREFERENCE FOR LIMITED
AND SHARED POWER

The tripartite system of *ketarim* (crowns of leadership), which has characterized Jewish communities since the biblical era, is predicated upon the idea that limiting and sharing power will avoid the scourges of autocracy and maximize the effective functioning of a community. The highly selective nature of today's Jewish world in which many are happily "picking and choosing" their way through the breadth and depth of the Jewish experience only underscores the wisdom of this ancient system and the importance of returning to it. Now, more than ever, it is essential that each of the ketaric functions—educational, religious/spiritual, and political—be strengthened and reinvigorated, since, today, most Jews will only opt to explore a single "slice" of Jewish life at any given time. Some, driven by a deep theological yearning, may seek to enter the Jewish experience through the portal of *keter kehunah*—the religious and spiritual realm. Others, motivated by an interest in social justice and a desire to heal the world through new forms of cutting-edge charitable work, will find opportunities in the world of *keter malkhut*—

the civic and political arena. The intellectually curious and academically oriented may choose to immerse themselves primarily in the *keter* of *torah*—the world of Jewish learning and study.

Only a system that insists on shared leadership can guarantee that each of the *ketarim* will be adaptable and accessible enough to provide today's Jews with equally inviting and compelling points of entry. Only a system that rejects the idea that one person or group can do it all will insist that a wide cross section of communal interests be represented at the table of communal discourse. Similarly, only a system built upon the virtues of shared and circumscribed power will consistently seek to nurture and train future generations of leaders. Because even the greatest individuals must limit their powers and because no single leader can ever expect to succeed in a vacuum, the traditional wisdom insists that the most important task any leader can perform is to empower and nurture the leadership potential of others.

To succeed with this eclectic generation then, twenty-first-century Jewish communal leaders will need to return to the behaviors and reembrace the precepts that have been considered essential for Jewish leaders throughout most of Jewish history. While the future is too uncertain to proffer ironclad predictions, a new cadre of lay and professional communal leaders crafted in the mold of the traditional insights described throughout this work, represents the best chance of responding to the challenges confronting Judaism and Jewish life in this new era.

NOTES

1. See for example, Sue Fishkoff, "Jews Looking Outside Synagogues for New Rituals and Life-Cycle Events," *Jewish Telegraphic Association*, October 10, 2005, jta.org/page_view_story.asp?intarticleid = 15932&intcategoryid = 4 (11 Oct. 2005). Also see Sue Fishkoff, "Young U.S. Jews Find Offbeat Ways to Express Identity," *Jerusalem Post*, September 28, 2005, www.jpost.com/servlet/Satellite?pagename = JPost/JPArticle/Show Full&cid = 112770120653 (29 Sept. 2005); and Steven M. Cohen and Arnold M. Eisen, *The Jew Within* (Bloomington: Indiana University Press, 2000).

2. Jonathan D. Sarna, *American Judaism* (New Haven, CT: Yale University Press, 2004), 373.

3. Jonathan D. Sarna, "The Ever-Vanishing American Jew," *Jerusalem Post*, June 3, 2004, www.jpost.com/servlet/Satellite?pagename = Jpost/JPArticle/ShowFull&cid = 10 86230742043&p = 1006953079865 (4 Jun. 2004).

4. *Sotah* 37a.

5. Genesis Rabbah 80:1. Reflecting a similar sentiment, the second president of the United States, John Adams, once wrote, "If worthless men are sometimes at the head of affairs, it is, I believe because worthless men are in the tail and the middle." See David McCullough, *John Adams* (New York: Simon and Schuster, 2001), 591.

Chapter Nine

A Final Reflection

As I have sought to make clear in this book, Judaism offers a definitive view as to what it means to be an effective leader. It is a view honed over centuries that is at the same time profoundly idealistic and abundantly pragmatic. It is deeply rooted, yet adaptable; fixed, yet flexible. It addresses people's spiritual yearnings and political realities. Notably, the enduring principles of these centuries-old Jewish writings on power, authority, decision-making, succession planning, and related issues are today being advanced as among the most progressive theories on leadership. As demonstrated, long before Warren Bennis declared the end of the "Great Man," and Jim Collins revealed the potency of the "Level 5" leader, the Torah insisted that leadership belonged to the many, not the few, and that a leader's efficacy depends upon the ability to combine tenacity with humility. Similarly, before Ronald Heifetz and Marty Linsky demanded that leaders take stock of their own behaviors by honestly asking what their "piece of the mess" has been, ancient Jewish sources insisted that no leader can presume to lead unless he or she has first acknowledged and then repented personal mistakes. And before Robert Greenleaf introduced the power of "servant leadership," the Bible and rabbinic texts required all communal heads to think of themselves as serving, not ruling.

Furthermore, there is evidence that venerable entities from the U.S. military to corporate America are today embracing conceptions of power and leadership that share much in common with classical Jewish precepts on the subject. When today's army instructs its officers that above all else "you must develop character and competence" and "take care of your people";[1] or when Jeffrey Immelt, chairman of General Electric, declares that if you want to be a great company you first have to be a good company;[2] when eBay's Meg Whitman speaks of executive leadership as "a span of influence, not of control";[3] or when other corporations, from Southwest Airlines to Ben and Jerry's and Starbucks, seek to emphasize the "spiritual dimension" in business and speak proudly of "doing well by doing good" or of providing "good value" because of their company's "good values," something significant is happening.[4] To be sure, these declarations can easily be dismissed as marketing hype. But, even if that is the case, these "new" messages are designed to motivate a public that has very little confidence in current leadership and is desperately seeking a radically different type of leader from the bloviating, arrogant, macho man of the past.

According to a study on "Confidence in Leadership," conducted by Yankelovich, Inc., in partnership with *U.S. News & World Report* and the Center for Public Leadership at the John F. Kennedy School of Government at Harvard University in September of 2005, most Americans believe that their leaders cannot be trusted, are out of touch, and have been corrupted by their own power. Fully 95 percent of Americans say what they want most from their leaders is honesty and integrity followed by effective communication. Importantly, substantial numbers of Americans (82 percent) are willing to acknowledge that they, as followers, share some of the blame for this current crisis in leadership.[5]

When evaluated in light of the sources presented in this book, the results of this study suggest that Judaism's conception of effective leadership has much to teach and contribute to the general population. The message of shared and circumscribed power and of humble leaders who take responsibility for their actions, apologize for their mistakes, and combine competence with character is a potent one, indeed. The idea that a leader's success is linked to his or her ability to nurture the leadership capacity in others has enormous ramifications within and beyond the Jewish world. So, too, for Judaism's insights into the reciprocal role that followers must play in order to elevate the efficacy of their leaders.

It is particularly ironic, therefore, in an era in which Judaism's classical insights are desperately needed, and regularly validated, that large numbers of Jewish groups and organizations remain unaware of the wisdom of their own tradition. It rarely occurs to them, as they zealously seek "outside" expertise for the development of their boards, officers, young "leaders," and professionals, that the very theories and approaches touted by management specialists and business school professors are often built upon the venerable teachings of Judaism.

In large measure, the goal of this book has been to introduce Jewish leaders to Judaism's views on leadership. Whether one feels bound to incorporate all of these insights into a personal leadership style is not the point. Nor has the goal been to dismiss other approaches to leadership as second-rate. Rather, it is enough that those who think of themselves and who are looked upon as

Jewish leaders, whether in a local synagogue or on an international board of governors, become familiar with and consider the applicability of these classical precepts. Their potency and relevance will speak for themselves.

NOTES

1. *Army Leadership—Be, Know, Do*, Field Manual No. 22–100 (Washington, DC: 1999), 1–2.

2. Thomas L. Friedman, *The World Is Flat: A Brief History of the Twenty-first Century* (New York: Farrar, Straus & Giroux, 2005), 302.

3. William Meyers, "Keeping A Gentle Grip on Power," *U.S. News & World Report*, 31 October 2005, 78.

4. See Lee G. Bolman and Terrence E. Deal, *Reframing Organizations: Artistry, Choice, and Leadership* (San Francisco: Jossey-Bass, 1997), 340–44. Also see William Meyers, "Conscience in a Cup of Coffee," *U.S. News & World Report*, 31 October 2005, 48–50.

5. *National Leadership Index 2005: A National Study of Confidence in Leadership*, October 18, 2005 www.usnews.com/usnews/news/features/051022/22leaders.pdf (23 Nov. 2005).

Bibliography

Army Leadership—Be, Know, Do. Field Manual No. 22–100. Washington, DC, 1999.

Baron, Salo. *The Jewish Community*. Three Volumes. Philadelphia: The Jewish Publication Society of America, 1948.

Baum, Herb. "Transparent Leadership." *Leader to Leader* no. 37 (Summer 2005): 41–47.

Bell, Chip R. "The Vulnerable Leader." *Leader to Leader* no. 38 (Fall 2005): 19–23.

Bell, Dean Phillip. *Sacred Communities: Jewish and Christian Identities in Fifteenth-Century Germany*. Boston and Leiden: Brill Academic Publishers, Inc., 2001.

Bennis, Warren. *On Becoming a Leader*. New York: Basic Books, 2003.

Bennis, Warren G., and Robert J. Thomas. *Geeks and Geezers—How Era, Values, and Defining Moments Shape Leaders*. Boston: Harvard Business School Press, 2002.

Ben-Sasson, Haim Hillel. "The Middle Ages." Pp. 385–723 in *A History of the Jewish People*, edited by H. H. Ben-Sasson. Cambridge, MA: Harvard University Press, 1976.

Bettan, Israel. *Studies in Jewish Preaching*. Cincinnati: Hebrew Union College Press, 1939.

Blenkinsopp, Joseph. *Sage, Priest, Prophet: Religious and Intellectual Leadership in Ancient Israel*. Louisville, KY: Westminster John Knox Press, 1995.

Blidstein, Gerald J. "Individual and Community in the Middle Ages: *Halakhic* Theory." Pp. 327–69 in *Kinship and Consent: The Jewish Political Tradition and Its Contemporary Uses*, edited by Daniel J. Elazar. New Brunswick, NJ: Transaction Publishers, 1997.

Bolman, Lee G., and Terrence E. Deal. *Reframing Organizations: Artistry, Choice, and Leadership*. San Francisco: Jossey-Bass, 1997.

Bonfil, Robert. *Rabbis and Jewish Communities in Renaissance Italy*. London: The Littman Library of Jewish Civilization, 1993.

Borowitz, Eugene. "*Tzimtzum*: A Mystic Model for Contemporary Leadership," Pp. 331–41 in *What We Know About Jewish Education: A Handbook of Today's Research for Tomorrow's Jewish Education*, edited by Stuart L. Kelman. Los Angeles: Torah Aura Productions, 1992.

Bryman, Alan. *Charisma and Leadership in Organizations*. London: Sage Publications, 1992.

Buber, Martin. *Tales of the Hasidim—Early Masters*. New York: Schocken Books, 1947.

———. *Tales of the Hasidim—Later Masters*. New York: Schocken Books, 1948.

Bubis, Gerald B. "Brokha Brokers and Power Brokers." *Jewish Spectator* 40, no. 1 (Spring 1975): 9–12.

———. ed. *The Director Had a Heart Attack and the President Resigned—Board-Staff Relations for the 21st Century.* Jerusalem: Jerusalem Center for Public Affairs, 1999.

———. "Present Realities and Future Possibilities." Pp. 5–73 in *The Director Had a Heart Attack and the President Resigned—Board-Staff Relations for the 21st Century,* edited by Gerald B. Bubis. Jerusalem: Jerusalem Center for Public Affairs, 1999.

Bubis, Gerald B., and Steven M. Cohen. "American Jewish Leaders View Board-Staff Relations." Pp. 87–131 in *The Director Had a Heart Attack and the President Resigned—Board-Staff Relations for the 21st Century,* edited by Gerald B. Bubis. Jerusalem: Jerusalem Center for Public Affairs, 1999.

Bubis, Gerald B., and Steven Windmueller. *From Predictability to Chaos?? How Jewish Leaders Reinvented Their National Communal System.* Baltimore: Center for Jewish Community Studies, 2005.

Burns, James MacGregor. *Leadership.* New York: HarperCollins, 1978.

Carlyle, Thomas. *On Heroes, Hero-Worship and the Heroic in History.* Lincoln: University of Nebraska Press, 1966.

Cohen, Steven M., and Arnold M. Eisen. *The Jew Within.* Bloomington: Indiana University Press, 2000.

Cohen, Stuart A. "The Concept of the Three *Ketarim*: Their Place in Jewish Political Thought and Implications for Studying Jewish Constitutional History." Pp. 47–76 in *Kinship and Consent: The Jewish Political Tradition and Its Contemporary Uses,* edited by Daniel J. Elazar. New Brunswick: Transaction Publishers, 1997.

Collins, Jim. *Good to Great: Why Some Companies Make the Leap . . . and Others Don't.* New York: HarperBusiness, 2001.

———. "Level 5 Leadership: The Triumph of Humility and Fierce Resolve." Reprint. *Harvard Business Review* (January 2001).

Conger, Jay A. *Learning to Lead: The Art of Transforming Managers into Leaders.* San Francisco: Jossey-Bass, 1992.

Conger, Jay A., and Beth Benjamin. *Building Leaders—How Successful Companies Develop the Next Generation.* San Francisco: Jossey-Bass, 1990.

Dresner, Samuel H. *The Zaddik.* Northvale, NJ: Jason Aronson, Inc., 1994.

Elazar, Daniel J. *Kinship and Consent: The Jewish Political Tradition and Its Contemporary Uses.* New Brunswick, NJ: Transaction Publishers, 1997.

Elazar, Daniel J., and Stuart A. Cohen. *The Jewish Polity: Jewish Political Organization from Biblical Times to the Present.* Bloomington: Indiana University Press, 1985.

Elon, Menachem. *Jewish Law—History, Sources, Principles.* Three Volumes. Philadelphia: The Jewish Publication Society, 1994.

———. "On Power and Authority: The *Halakhic* Source of the Traditional Community and Its Contemporary Implications." Pp. 293–326 in *Kinship and Consent: The Jewish Political Tradition and Its Contemporary Uses,* edited by Daniel J. Elazar. New Brunswick, NJ: Transaction Publishers, 1997.

Fairhurst, G. T., and R. A. Sarr. *The Art of Framing: Managing the Language of Leadership.* San Francisco: Jossey-Bass, 1996.

Finkelstein, Louis. *Jewish Self-Government in the Middle Ages.* New York: Phillip Feldheim, Inc., 1964.

Fishkoff, Sue. "Jews Looking Outside Synagogues For New Rituals and Life-Cycle Events." *Jewish Telegraphic Association.* October 10, 2005. jta.org/page_view_story .asp?intarticleid = 15932&intcategoryid = 4 (11 Oct. 2005).

———. "Young U.S. Jews Find Offbeat Ways to Express Identity." *Jerusalem Post.* September 28, 2005. www.jpost/com/servlet/Satellite&pagename = JPost/JPArticle/Show Full&cid = 1127701206523 (29 Sept. 2005).

Friedman, Thomas L. *The World Is Flat: A Brief History of the Twenty-first Century.* New York: Farrar, Straus, & Giroux, 2005.

Gaon, Saadia. *The Book of Beliefs and Opinions.* Translated by Samuel Rosenblatt. New Haven: Yale University Press, 1948.

Gergen, David. *Eyewitness to Power.* New York: Simon and Schuster, 2000.

Giber, David, Louis Carter, and Marshall Goldsmith, eds. *Best Practices in Leadership Development Handbook.* San Francisco: Jossey-Bass/Pfeiffer, 2000.

Goleman, Daniel. "The Emotional Intelligence of Leaders." Pp. 29–40 in *On Mission and Leadership,* edited by Frances Hesselbein and Rob Johnston. San Francisco: Jossey-Bass, 2002.

———. "What Makes A Leader?" Reprint. *Harvard Business Review* (November-December 1998): 93–102.

Green, Arthur. "Typologies of Leadership and the Hasidic Zaddiq." Pp. 127–56 in *Jewish Spirituality from the Sixteenth-century Revival to the Present,* edited by Arthur Green. New York: Crossroad, 1989.

Greenleaf Center for Servant-Leadership, "What is Servant-Leadership?" www.green leaf.org/leadership/servant-leadership/What-is-Servant-Leadership.html (29 Aug. 2005).

Greenleaf, Robert K. *Servant Leadership: A Journey into the Nature of Legitimate Power and Greatness.* New York: Paulist Press, 1977.

Heifetz, Ronald A. *Leadership Without Easy Answers.* Cambridge, MA: Harvard University Press, 1994.

Heifetz, Ronald A., and Marty Linsky. *Leadership on the Line.* Boston: Harvard Business School Press, 2002.

Herold, J. C., ed. *The Mind of Napoleon: A Selection from His Written and Spoken Words.* New York: Columbia University Press, 1955.

Heschel, Abraham J. *The Prophets.* New York: Perennial Classics, 2001.

Horowitz, Carmi. *The Jewish Sermon in 14th Century Spain: The Derashot of R. Joshua ibn Shu'eib.* Cambridge, MA: Harvard University Press, 1989.

Hutton, Rodney R. *Charisma and Authority in Israelite Society.* Minneapolis: Fortress Press, 1994.

Jablin, Frederic M. "Communication." Pp. 222–27 in *Encyclopedia of Leadership,* edited by George R. Goethals, Georgia J. Sorenson, and James MacGregor Burns. Thousand Oaks, CA: Sage Publications, 2004.

Jacobs, Louis. *Jewish Values.* Hartford: Hartmore House, Inc., 1960.

Karlgaard, Rich. "Peter Drucker on Leadership." *Forbes* 2004. www.forbes.com/2004/ 11/19cz_rk_1110drucker_print.html (8 Aug. 2005).

Katz, Jacob. *Tradition and Crisis—Jewish Society at the End of the Middle Ages.* Translated by Bernard Cooperman. New York: Schocken Books, 1993.

Kelley, Robert E. "In Praise of Followers." Reprint, *Harvard Business Review* (November–December 1988).

Kotter, John P. "What Leaders Really Do." Pp. 37–60 in *On Leadership*, Harvard Business Review. Boston: Harvard Business School Publishing, 1990.

Kouzes, James M., and Barry Z. Posner. *The Leadership Challenge*. San Francisco: Jossey-Bass, 1995.

Lamm, Norman. *The Religious Thought of Hasidism*. New York: Yeshiva University Press, 1999.

Lencioni, Patrick. *The Five Dysfunctions of a Team*. San Francisco: Jossey-Bass, 2002.

Lerner, Michael. *Jewish Renewal*. New York: HarperCollins, 1994.

Lewis, Hal M. "Making Leaders: How the American Jewish Community Prepares Its Lay Leaders." *Journal of Jewish Communal Service* 80, no. 2–3 (Summer/Fall 2004): 151–59.

———. *Models and Meanings in the History of Jewish Leadership*. Lewiston, NY: The Edwin Mellen Press, 2004.

Ludwig, Arnold M. *King of the Mountain*. Lexington: The University Press of Kentucky, 2002.

McCullough, David. *John Adams*. New York: Simon and Schuster, 2001.

Marcus, Ivan G. "Judah the Pietist and Eleazar of Worms: From Charismatic to Conventional Leadership." Pp. 97–126 in *Jewish Mystical Leaders and Leadership in the 13th Century*, edited by Moshe Idel and Mortimer Ostow. Northvale, NJ: Jason Aronson Inc., 1998.

———. *Piety and Society: The Jewish Pietists of Medieval Germany*. Leiden: E. J. Brill, 1981.

Meyers, William. "Conscience in a Cup of Coffee." *U.S. News & World Report* (31 October 2005): 48–50.

———. "Keeping A Gentle Grip on Power." *U.S. News & World Report* (31 October 2005): 78–80.

Nadler, David A. *Champions of Change: How CEOs and Their Companies Are Mastering the Skills of Radical Change*. San Francisco: Jossey-Bass, 1997.

Nadler, David A., Robert B. Shaw, and A. Elise Walton. *Discontinuous Change: Leading Organizational Transformation*. San Francisco: Jossey-Bass, 1995.

National Leadership Index 2005: A National Study of Confidence in Leadership (18 October 2005) www.usnews.com/usnews/news/features/051022/22leaders.pdf (23 Nov. 2005).

Netanyahu, B. *Don Isaac Abravanel*. Philadelphia: The Jewish Publication Society of America, 1982.

Newman, Louis I. *Hasidic Anthology*. New York: Schocken Books, 1963.

Pawel, Ernst. *The Labyrinth of Exile*. New York: Farrar, Straus & Giroux, 1980.

Rabbi-Congregation Relationship: A Vision for the 21st Century. Philadelphia: Reconstructionist Commission on the Role of the Rabbi, 2001.

Saperstein, Marc, ed. *Essential Papers on Messianic Movements and Personalities in Jewish History*. New York: New York University Press, 1992.

Sarna, Jonathan D. *American Judaism*. New Haven: Yale University Press, 2004.

———. "The Ever-Vanishing American Jew," *Jerusalem Post*. June 3, 2004. www.jpost.com/servlet/Satellite?pagename = Jpost/JPArticle/ShowFull&cid = 1086230742043& p = 1006953079865 (4 Jun . 2004).

Schwarz, Sidney. *Finding a Spiritual Home—How a New Generation of Jews Can Transform the American Synagogue*. New York: John Wiley & Sons, Inc., 2000.

Schwarzfuchs, Simon. *A Concise History of the Rabbinate*. Oxford: Blackwell, 1993.

Senge, Peter M. "Missing the Boat on Leadership." *Leader to Leader* no. 38 (Fall 2005): 28–30.

Sharot, Stephen. *Messianism, Mysticism, and Magic*. Chapel Hill: University of North Carolina Press, 1982.

Sherwin, Byron L. *Mystical Theology and Social Dissent*. London: Associated University Presses, 1982.

————. *Workers of Wonders*. Lanham, MD: Rowman & Littlefield Publishers, Inc., 2004.

Sherwin, Byron L., and Seymour J. Cohen. *How To Be A Jew*. Northvale, NJ: Jason Aronson Inc., 1992.

Siddur Sim Shalom. New York: The Rabbinical Assembly, 1985.

Sippurei Besht. Warsaw: A J. Kleiman, 1911.

Spinoza, Baruch. *Tractatus Theologico-Politicus*. Translated by Samuel Shirley. Leiden: E. J. Brill, 1991.

Stogdill, R. M. "Personal Factors Associated with Leadership." *Journal of Psychology* no. 25 (1948): 35–71.

Swetschinski, Daniel M. *Reluctant Cosmopolitans: The Portuguese Jews of Seventeenth-Century Amsterdam*. London: The Littman Library of Jewish Civilization, 2000.

Tannenbaum, Robert, and Warren H. Schmidt. "How to Choose a Leadership Pattern." Reprint. *Harvard Business Review* (May–June 1973): 3–12.

Telushkin, Joseph. *Jewish Humor: What the Best Jewish Jokes Say About the Jews*. New York: William Morrow and Company, Inc., 1992.

Tichy, Noel M., and Stratford Sherman. *Control Your Destiny or Someone Else Will*. New York: HarperCollins Publishers, 1993.

United Jewish Communities. *The National Jewish Population Survey 2000–01: Strength, Challenge and Diversity in the American Jewish Population*. New York: United Jewish Communities, 2003.

Walzer, Michael, Menachem Lorberbaum, and Noam J. Zohar, eds. *The Jewish Political Tradition*. Two Volumes. New Haven: Yale University Press, 2000.

Weber, Max. *The Theory of Social and Economic Organization*. Translated by A. M. Henderson and Talcott Parsons. New York: The Free Press, 1947.

Wildavsky, Aaron. *The Nursing Father*. Tuscaloosa: The University of Alabama Press, 1984.

Wilson, Robert A., ed. *Character Above All*. New York: Touchstone, 1995.

Yukl, Gary. *Leadership in Organizations*. Upper Saddle River, NJ: Prentice Hall, 2002.

Zaleznik, Abraham. "Managers and Leaders—Are They Different?" Pp. 61–88 in *On Leadership*, Harvard Business Review. Boston: Harvard Business School Publishing, 1990.

Zander, Rosamund Stone, and Benjamin Zander. *The Art of Possibility*. Boston: Harvard Business School Press, 2000.

Zeitlin, Solomon. "Rashi and the Rabbinate." *Jewish Quarterly Review* Volume 31 (1940–41): 1–58.

Zimmer, Eric. *Harmony and Discord: An Analysis of the Decline of Jewish Self-Government in 15th Century Central Europe*. New York: Yeshiva University Press, 1970.

Zivotofsky, Ari Z. "The Leadership Qualities of Moses." *Judaism* (Summer 1994): 258–69.

Index

About the Author

Hal M. Lewis is Associate Professor of Contemporary Jewish Studies and Dean of Public Programming at Spertus Institute of Jewish Studies in Chicago. An experienced organizational executive, he is the author of *Models and Meanings in the History of Jewish Leadership* and many essays on leadership and the contemporary Jewish community.